CONGRESS AND
THE BUDGET

CONGRESS AND THE BUDGET

Joel Havemann

INDIANA UNIVERSITY PRESS
Bloomington & London

Manufactured in the United States of America

Library of Congress Cataloging in Publication Data

Havemann, Joel
    Congress and the budget.

    Bibliography:
    Includes index.
    1. Budget—United States.   I. Title.
HJ2052.H38   353.007'22   78-1851
ISBN 0-253-31406-2   1 2 3 4 5 82 81 80 79 78

CONTENTS

PREFACE

IT'S BEEN JUST three years since they were two brand-new committees with vague and untested powers, supported by a staff office that still didn't exist. My most vivid memories of the House and Senate Budget Committees and the Congressional Budget Office in those early days are of their least auspicious moments. Of members of the Senate Budget Committee, unsure whether social security and revenue sharing were part of the federal budget. Of House Budget Committee members, determined to balance the budget without delay but arguing whether to cut defense or revenue sharing or welfare or law enforcement assistance. Of the director of the CBO, after her belated appointment, introduced to the press by Budget Committee chairmen who disagreed sharply over her duties. These were the instruments that would redress the balance of budgetary power between Congress and the president? That would introduce fiscal responsibility to the legislative branch?

The Budget Committees, with the CBO's help, have come a long way in three years. They know now that social security and revenue sharing are indeed part of the budget. They realize that spending cuts alone can't balance the budget; there also must be an improved national economy. They also know that they can wield a certain—if limited—influence over the size and shape of the federal budget. They haven't balanced the budget, and they haven't reordered spending priorities. But at least they have consistently made Comgress aware of the effect of its action on total federal spending and the deficit.

Assigned by *National Journal* to congressional budget reform since its enactment in 1974, I have followed the Budget

Committees' ups and downs from the beginning. That experience has been vital to the writing of this book; so have the friends who have advised me on all or part of its contents. Robert J. Samuelson of *National Journal,* one of Washington's finest economic journalists, helped me shape my conclusions about the congressional budget process and put them into a more logical and readable form than I could have provided alone. Lauren J. Walters, law student, consultant to northeast governors, and a member of the original Senate Budget Committee staff, read the entire manuscript, adding insights and correcting errors. Thanks also to others who helped with individual chapters—Sara Fitzgerald of *National Journal,* Mark Gordon of the Senate Appropriations Committee staff, and Johnny K. Alexander of the University of Cincinnati.

I am also grateful for the continuing cooperation of the participants in the budget process: Edmund Muskie, Henry Bellmon, and the members of the Senate Budget Committee; Al Ullman, Brock Adams, Robert Giaimo, and the members of the House Budget Committee; Alice Rivlin and her staff at the Congressional Budget Office; Doug Bennet, John McEvoy, Bob Boyd, Sid Brown, and the staff of the Senate Budget Committee; and Walter Kravitz, George Gross, Bruce Meredith and the House Budget Committee staff. Budget officers are never very popular, and the Budget Committees and the CBO aren't everybody's favorites on Capitol Hill. But they are mine.

Joel Havemann
Washington, January 1978

CONGRESS AND
THE BUDGET

CHAPTER 1

THE ROOTS OF BUDGET
REFORM

OF ALL THE POWERS that the Constitution conferred on Congress, none proved so overrated for so long as the power over the purse. "The Congress shall have power," the Constitution declared, "to lay and collect taxes, duties, imposts and excises, to pay the debts and provide for the common defense and general welfare of the United States."[1] In the Federalist Papers, Alexander Hamilton predicted that this power would allow Congress to overcome "all the overgrown prerogatives of the other branches of the government. This power over the purse may, in fact, be regarded as the most complete and effectual weapon with which any constitution can arm the immediate representatives of the people."[2]

It didn't work out that way. As the federal budget grew to sizes that Hamilton could never have imagined, Congress divided responsibility for the budget among nearly all of its committees. Authority over taxes fell in one committee in the House and another in the Senate, but these committees did not decide whether the government should live within or beyond its means. Spending jurisdiction lay elsewhere—some of it divided among thirteen appropriations committees in each chamber, the rest split among ten or fifteen other committees. Spending bills came to votes on the House and Sen-

ate floors individually, over a period of many months every
year. Many became law after the budget year had begun. In
the meantime, the affected government agencies had to limp
along with emergency funds that they could spend at last
year's pace. In 1974, Sen. Sam J. Ervin, Jr., described the
chaos that was congressional budget-making:

> Congress never decides how much total expenditures should
> be, nor does it go on record as to whether the budget should
> have a surplus or a deficit. The total seems to just happen,
> without anyone being responsible for it, or knowing with much
> confidence what it will be.[3]

In contrast, the president managed the federal budget with
strict control. His Office of Management and Budget (OMB),[4]
an organization of some six hundred of Washington's best
bureaucrats, helped him mold the spending demands of all
the executive branch departments and agencies into a single,
coherent proposal reflecting his economic policies and political priorities. His annual budget recommendation to Congress, as Sen. Charles H. Percy found in 1974, "hits Congress
each year like a tidal wave."[5] Lacking any mechanism of central budget control, Congress could do little more than tinker
with the president's proposals around the edges, adding some
here, cutting a little there. It could not possibly substitute its
own economic policies or spending priorities for those of the
president, at least not in any deliberate way. And when President Nixon impounded—that is, refused to spend—funds
that Congress had voted for particular programs, Congress
found itself helpless to determine even the individual components of the budget. The Constitution notwithstanding, Congress had yielded its power over the purse to the president.
Finally, in 1974, Congress mustered the will to assert its
constitutional authority. The Congressional Budget and Impoundment Control Act, or the budget reform act, as the
1974 law will be called, required Congress twice each year to
do what it had never done before—to decide the totals of the

federal budget. The congressional budget, in the form of a resolution that would not require presidential signature, would spell out total federal spending and revenue—with the resulting surplus or deficit—for the coming budget year. In addition, it would divide spending among sixteen broad national priorities, such as defense, health, and income security.

The first resolution each year, to be voted in May, would set targets that Congress would try to hit as it proceeded to enact individual spending and revenue bills for the coming year. The second resolution, scheduled for September, would modify the targets and turn them into upper limits on spending and a lower limit on revenue. The budget reform act changed the first day of the fiscal year—the twelve months for which budget measures have effect—from July 1 to October 1. By October 1, if Congress held to its budget schedule, all spending and revenue legislation would be in place for the new year.

The budget resolutions would be prepared by new Budget Committees in the House and Senate. The taxing and spending committees of Congress would continue to perform their traditional functions; the Budget Committees would simply help Congress construct the framework into which individual pieces of legislation should fit. The Budget Committees would be assisted by a third new institution, a Congressional Budget Office, a source of budgetary expertise that would break Congress's dependence on the executive branch for information relating to the budget.

THE FORCES FOR DECENTRALIZATION

The federal budget, which totaled only $1.4 million in the republic's first year, remained relatively manageable through the nineteenth century, growing only to $521 million, or 3 percent of the national economy, by 1900. Then the budget took off. Two World Wars and conflicts in Korea and Vietnam forced enormous temporary increases in spending. More significantly, the social programs that began with Roosevelt's New Deal and multiplied during Johnson's Great Society added permanent outlays to the federal budget. By the end of the Korean War, the budget absorbed fully 20 percent of the nation's output, a level around which it fluctuated through the 1970s. But in absolute magnitude, the budget continued to grow with breathtaking speed, surpassing $250 billion in 1974.

As the budget grew, it became an increasingly significant influence on the nation's economy. John Maynard Keynes, the British economist, demonstrated as early as 1936 that manipulation of the size of the budget—and its surplus or deficit— could moderate the pernicious cycle of boom and bust that had plunged western nations into the Depression. A strong dose of federal spending, accompanied by a deficit, could cure a recession, according to Keynesian theory, while a surplus could dampen an overheated economy and temper inflation. Keynesian economic theory came unglued in the late 1960s and early 1970s, when inflation and recession coexisted. But most economists still regarded fiscal policy—the use of the budget to regulate the economy—as an indispensable tool in preventing those twin evils.

Equally important, shaping the enormous federal budget meant determining the spending priorities for the nation's single biggest pot of money. The government had the power to decide how many billions of dollars should support defense and how many should support the poor. It could shift huge sums from the space program to highway construction, from urban development to foreign aid.

But as the federal budget grew ever larger and more complicated, Congress followed the natural tendency to divide budget responsibility among its various committees. Decentralization began in 1865, when the House of Representatives decided to break up its Ways and Means Committee, which had been in charge of all matters relating to the federal Treasury since the early days of the republic. The Ways and Means

Committee's job became increasingly burdensome as the Civil War drove the federal budget up to $800 million—a sum that Rep. Samuel S. Cox found to be "stupendous." Cox felt the House should create a new committee to assume responsibility for the spending side of the budget so that the Ways and Means Committee could specialize in taxes.[6] Not all his colleagues agreed; Rep. DeWitt Clinton Littlejohn warned the House:

> The merchant prince of New York, transacting commerce with all parts of the globe, must have before him every day his assets and income, in order that he may understand how to meet his obligations. So too with your Committee of Ways and Means. . . . No committee can make appropriations unless it has before it the income of the government for the fiscal year; . . . else there might be a year when your appropriations would exceed very largely the amount provided to carry on the government.[7]

But Littlejohn's prophecy, so appropriate to the 1970s, went unheeded, and the House Appropriations Committee was born. Two years later the Senate did the same, separating an Appropriations Committee from its Finance Committee. More than a century would pass before individual committees of the House and Senate would look at revenues and expenditures simultaneously.

In their first twenty years, the Appropriations Committees wielded great power and aroused fierce jealousies among the rest of the House and Senate. In 1885, Rep. William M. Springer denounced House Appropriations Committee members as an "honored few in our midst." The committee, he complained, "has more business committed to it than it is possible for any fifteen members of this House to properly consider and mature in the little time allowed them by laws."[8] The House Rules Committee proposed to strip the Appropriations Committee of control over six important bills, including military spending, and reassign the power to authorizing

committees—those that prepare legislation authorizing programs whose funds are provided in subsequent appropriations bills. Rep. Samuel J. Randall argued that the House was
compounding the mistake it had made in 1865, when it split
the Appropriations Committee from Ways and Means. "General appropriation bills are to be still further divided and
scattered," Randall warned, "and the result inevitably will be
that it will be impossible to keep any just relations between
receipts and expenditures."[9] But Randall's argument failed to
diminish the eagerness of House members who did not sit on
the Appropriations Committee to get a piece of the spending
action. The House dispersed its Appropriations Committee's
authority, and the Senate followed the same course in 1899.[10]

A sudden shift toward centralization followed World War
I, when the biggest deficits in the nation's history focused
attention on the management of the federal purse. In 1920,
Congress put its Appropriations Committees back in charge
of all appropriations bills. "We are trying to get away from the
practice of providing for a particular activity of the government with no relation at all to the other activities of the government," said Rep. Simeon D. Fess in language that would
not have been out of place in the 1970s.[11]

In the following year, Congress enacted the Budget and
Accounting Act of 1921, centralizing budget-making authority in the executive branch. Until then, each executive department and agency submitted its budget request directly to
Congress; the president had no way to organize their spending plans into a coherent package embodying his own policies. The Budget and Accounting Act established a Bureau of
the Budget in the Treasury Department—Franklin Roosevelt
moved it to the new Executive Office of the President in 1939
—to oversee all executive branch requests.

After the centralizing steps of 1920 and 1921, Congress
drifted gradually back in the other direction. Without disman-
tling its Appropriations Committees, as it had in the previous
century, Congress found new techniques for placing final

spending authority in the hands of other committees. In 1932 it authorized the Reconstruction Finance Corporation to borrow money directly from the Treasury; the economy-minded Appropriations Committees had no opportunity to cut the RFC's borrowing authority. And it passed legislation—social security in 1935 was an early example—that made permanent appropriations for programs entitling individuals to federal benefits. "Backdoor spending," the name for spending mandated without Appropriations Committee action, grew for forty years until it accounted for about one-third of the budget.

In 1946, Congress once again was propelled into action by the enormous deficits of the recent war. It created the Joint Economic Committee, whose members, from both the House and the Senate, would be responsible for studying the economy and the government's impact on it. But the new committee lacked authority to prepare legislation.

In that same year, another joint House-Senate committee, this one on the Organization of Congress, proposed a radical centralization of congressional budget-making. Congress, the joint committee argued, should look at the entire federal budget—revenue as well as spending—at one time, just as it had before 1865. Sen. Robert M. LaFollette, Jr., the joint committee's chairman, defended its proposal with language remarkably similar to that used by budget reformers twenty-eight years later:

> Although Congress is charged by the Constitution with the power of the purse, there is now no correlation between income and outgo. Taxes [are] levied and appropriations made by many separate committees. The right hand does not know what the left hand is doing.[12]

The vehicle of budget reform was to be an annual budget resolution in which Congress would set total federal spending and revenue for the coming year. But when the House and Senate first tried the new procedure in 1947, they failed to

agree on a budget resolution. The next year they adopted a
resolution but proceeded to enact spending and revenue bills
that violated it. After that, they simply ignored the budget
reform procedure of 1946 and reverted to their traditional,
piecemeal approach to the budget.

That approach, which by the 1970s had persisted for nearly
a century, certainly did not lack appeal. For one thing, it
allowed nearly all senators and representatives to exercise
control over particular segments of the budget. Members of
Congress drew their power from their seats on committees
that authorized programs and appropriated funds to operate
them. As long as most committees could control their own
pieces of the budget, most members could share in the opportunity to shape the budget. Senior members of important
committees, subject to no central budgetary control, could
wield decisive influence over programs in their committees'
jurisdiction.

In addition, Congress's lack of central control over the
budget enabled its members to concentrate on the specific,
narrow issues that were important to their constituents. Both
Congress and the public found it easier to understand the
pros and cons of the B-1 bomber or Medicaid than to grapple
with the intangible issues of fiscal policy and spending priorities. Many members of Congress believed they made friends
among the voters by supporting or opposing individual programs—by voting for federal aid for a highway back home, for
example, while opposing public service jobs for inner-city
teens.

Centralization, on the other hand, would force Congress to
face the budgetary consequences of all these individual
spending decisions, unpleasant though those consequences
might be. No longer would Congress enjoy the luxury of
voting for a popular new spending program, or for a tax cut,
without being aware of the impact on the overall budget.
Congress would have to face up to the federal deficit, which
grew to fantastic proportions in the 1970s. If Congress had

to adopt a budget, it would have to endorse a deficit—and no member of Congress relished putting his imprimatur on the deficits of $50 billion to $70 billion that became virtually inevitable in the economic circumstances of the 1970s.[13] Let the president make the tough, unpopular choices about total federal spending and revenue—and the deficit. Congress could be content to criticize the president's budget policy while leaving itself powerless to change it.

That argument held sway only as long as the president was willing to let Congress have the last word on the individual programs dear to the hearts of its members. But President Nixon was not. In 1972 and 1973, he resorted increasingly to impoundment—a presidential refusal to spend money that Congress had appropriated. Like Nixon, previous presidents had used impoundments, but they had done so with discretion. For the most part, they impounded money only when circumstances had changed after Congress made it available. But Nixon used impoundments to reduce or eliminate one program after another, on grounds that only the executive branch—and most emphatically not Congress—was capable of making the difficult choices about the budget. Only the executive branch, Nixon argued, could resist the pressures of the special interests for more spending programs. Only the executive branch could recognize that continuing federal deficits would lead to runaway inflation.

Impoundments hit Congress where it hurt. When Nixon said he was terminating programs that the nation could not afford, Congress had no response—because it had no way to prove him wrong. How could Congress weigh the advantages and disadvantages of including a particular program in the federal budget? It had no procedure for matching expenditures to revenues or for asking whether a new housing program, for example, was more important than a new submarine.

Congress could have instituted procedures to control presidential impoundments and let it go at that. But then how could it answer the inevitable critics—Nixon would have been the loudest—who would contend that Congress was letting spending grow out of control? How could Congress insist that the government spend money for a particular program without first setting an overall budget policy? Somebody had to manage the budget—and if Congress declined, the president would have to move in. If Congress was going to control presidential impoundments, it was going to have to control the federal budget at the same time.

CONGRESS AND THE PRESIDENT

The move in Congress to limit the use of impoundments represented a dramatic shift in relations between Congress and the White House. Just a decade before the 1974 budget reform act, the need for congressional procedures to check presidential powers would have seemed imcomprehensible. Popular opinion, shaped by the wisdom of the period's scholars, held Congress to be a den of villains bent on interfering with the white knight in the White House. Looking back at that period, historian Arthur M. Schlesinger, Jr., wrote: "Congress, it could be argued, had failed majority government in the high-technology society. It had proved itself incapable of the swift decisions demanded by the twentieth century. It could not make intelligent use of its war-making authority. It had no ordered means of setting national priorities or of controlling aggregate spending. It was not to be trusted with secrets. It was fragmented, parochial, selfish, cowardly, without dignity, discipline or purpose."[14]

In the liberal folklore of the time, the presidency was the salvation of American society. Bad presidents were not those who performed badly—that was not conceivable—but rather those who failed to use the power of their office to lead the nation toward solutions of its problems.[15] Political scientists fed a generation of students a diet of the glorified presidency. Clinton Rossiter, a leading rhetorician of the period, wrote:

All the massive political and social forces that brought the presidency to its present state of power and glory will continue to work in the future. Our economy and society will grow more rather than less interdependent, and we will turn to the president, anxiously if not always confidently, for help in solving the problems that fall thickly upon us. . . . And surely we have not seen our last great man in the White House.[16]

As Thomas E. Cronin wrote in 1970, "American young people grow up expecting their Presidents to be sufficiently powerful to win and end wars as well as cure the nation's socio-economic ills."[17]

The "uncritical cult of the activist presidency," as Schlesinger called it, permitted frequent unilateral presidential action, particularly in foreign affairs.[18] With Truman and Korea, Kennedy and the Cuban missile crisis, and Johnson and Vietnam, presidents acted largely on their own authority, with congressional acquiescence at most. That was all right in Korea and Cuba, but not in Vietnam, where Johnson did something the presidential cultists had not foreseen. He made a terrible mistake—not because he acted forcefully and unilaterally, but because his policies did not succeed.

If Johnson and Vietnam ignited the reaction against the imperial presidency, the Nixon years focused that reaction on domestic affairs. Nixon transferred an imperious style of conducting foreign affairs to many other spheres of activity as well. Impoundments were part of this pattern. In addition, Nixon refused to enforce certain civil rights laws. Stretching the doctrine of executive privilege, he refused to provide Congress with requested information. He used the CIA, FBI, and a special White House unit known as the "plumbers" to conduct political investigations, a transgression that ultimately led to Nixon's own downfall in the Watergate scandal.

But no matter how far down Watergate forced Nixon in public esteem, Congress continued to suffer from an even worse image. In January 1974, seven months before Nixon ignominiously left office, only 21 percent of the public gave

Congress a positive rating, compared with 30 percent for the president.[19] By the early 1970s, Congress sensed its impotence in relation to the White House—and the need to do something about it.

Overwhelmed by the resources at the disposal of the executive branch, Congress tried to improve its own capacity as a policy-making institution. The number of staff members assigned to committees, which were responsible for preparing most legislation, grew between 1960 and 1975 from about three hundred to 1,100 in the Senate and 450 to 1,700 in the House. More and more committees established oversight subcommittees to watch over the executive departments and agencies. To oversee a particularly sensitive sphere of executive branch activity, the Senate created its Select Intelligence Committee in 1976, and the House followed suit the following year. In 1972, Congress established the Office of Technology Assessment, a staff unit designed to provide Congress with "unbiased information concerning the physical, biological, economic, social and political effects" of congressional actions.[20]

With increasing frequency Congress enacted legislative vetoes that allowed it to block actions that the executive branch formerly would have had the power to take on its own. Thus Congress delegated to itself the power to approve the route of the Alaska oil pipeline and to overturn regulations of the Federal Election Commission. Congress enacted 163 legislative vetoes in the six years from 1970 through 1975, compared with just 132 such provisions between 1932, when the first one was enacted, and 1970.[21]

Sometimes Congress tried to increase its opportunities to formulate policy as well as block it. One important such effort was the 1973 War Powers Resolution, which was Congress's way of saying it was not going to watch any more Vietnams from the sidelines. Enacted over Nixon's veto, the resolution granted to Congress a form of legislative veto; the president could not commit troops to foreign combat for more than sixty days without specific congressional approval. But it also required the president to consult with Congress during military emergencies. In practice, however, this provision did little to advance Congress's chances to participate in the formulation of military policy. For example, President Ford found prompt consultation with Congress impossible during evacuation of the Da Nang military air base in South Vietnam; Congress was enjoying its Easter recess at the time, and Ford located the key members of military committees in twelve states, Mexico, Greece, the Middle East, and China.[22]

Of all the reactions to the imperial presidency, budget reform most effectively increased the opportunities for Congress not just to block presidential action but to make policy of its own. Only one feature of budget reform—impoundment control—took the form of a legislative veto designed to reduce the freedom of the president to take unilateral action. The bulk of the reform established procedures to enable Congress to approach the budget as a statement of economic policy and spending priorities. The Budget Committees and the Congressional Budget Office would become sources of budgetary information independent of the executive branch. Budget reform held the potential to make Congress a more effective policy-making body.

CONGRESSIONAL LEADERSHIP

Congress's traditional, decentralized approach to budget-making worked to the advantage of its committee chairmen, who enjoyed unchallenged control of the pieces of the budget under their committees' jusridiction. Already, the years between 1937 and 1971 have been called "the era of the committee chairmen."[23] It was an era symbolized by Rep. Howard W. Smith, the wily, archconservative Virginian who, as chairman of the House Rules Committee in the 1960s, could almost singlehandedly kill federal aid to education even though it was President Kennedy's first priority in domestic legislation. Smith, like his fellow committee chairmen, reached his position of leadership by virtue of his seniority on his committee. The seniority system had developed as an alternative to arbitrary appointment of committee chairmen by party leaders.

The years when congressional leaders could dominate through formal authority had ended in 1910, when the House stripped Speaker Joseph G. Cannon of his chairmanship of the Rules Committee and his power to appoint Rules Committee members. But, by the 1970s, even the dispersal of power to the committee chairmen failed to satisfy less senior senators and representatives, who demanded a bigger share of the legislative action for themselves. More liberal members of Congress felt particularly frustrated by the southern Democrats who controlled many of the key subcommittees throughout the House and cut into the powers of committee chairmen.[24] The seniority system was toppled in the House after the 1974 elections brought seventy-five new Democrats, many of them young and independent of their party's machinery, to Washington. When the 94th Congress opened in 1975, House Democrats replaced southerners with northerners in the chairs of the Agriculture, Armed Services, and Banking Committees. Wilbur D. Mills of Arkansas, the victim of a sex and alcohol scandal, stepped down voluntarily from Ways and Means. Other chairmen held on, but they realized that for the first time their survival depended on their performance.

Dethroning committee chairmen may have been an intoxicating experience for junior members of Congress, but the revolt against seniority also helped create a congressional power vacuum; it came during a period when more democratic leaders had replaced strong, autocratic leaders in both the House and the Senate. Lyndon B. Johnson, described as "the most effective majority leader to serve in recent times" in the Senate, became vice president in 1961.[25] A few months later, Sam Rayburn, one of the most forceful and persuasive of all House speakers and Johnson's mentor, died. Johnson and Rayburn had known how to dispense favors and cash in credits; they had been masters at reaching compromises and striking bargains.[26] But Johnson was replaced by Mike Mansfield, who would say upon retirement in 1976 that "the leadership subordinates itself to the will of the majority."[27] Rayburn was followed first by John W. McCormack and in 1971 by Carl Albert, both of whom, like Mansfield, were far less forceful than their predecessor. The shift in leadership style, coupled with the subsequent demise of the seniority system in the House, left Congress floundering.

To compensate, Congress turned not to individuals as before, but to new sets of institutions and procedures. Most of the new efforts aimed at centralization of power. In 1974, the House modified its committees' jurisdictions—although by much less than reformers had sought—in an attempt to make them coincide more closely with the issues that confronted Congress. One of the 1974 jurisdictional reforms, the shift of authority over revenue sharing from the overworked Ways and Means Committee to the Government Operations Committee, was an example of the effort to make the House a more efficient body. Because the 1974 reform failed to consolidate jurisdiction over energy policy, which had been scattered among about a dozen committees and subcommittees, the House in 1977 established an Ad Hoc Select Energy Committee to coordinate legislation in that area. In that same year, the Senate streamlined its committees' jurisdictions somewhat, although, like the House, it was unwilling to tamper as much with committee turf as some reformers had proposed.

Budget reform may be viewed as part of this drive toward internal congressional organization. The budget reform act did not cut into the jurisdiction of any of the dozen committees in the House and Senate that shared responsibility for legislation related to the federal budget. But it established Budget Committees to help Congress fit all that legislation into the mold of a coherent budget policy.

MEASURING THE SUCCESS OF
BUDGET REFORM

It may have been a bit of an exaggeration to say, as Senator Ervin once did, that budget reform was "one of the most important pieces of legislation that Congress has considered since the first Congress."[28] But there was no doubt that budget reform was going to have enormous impact on both the operation of Congress and the government's fiscal policy and spending priorities. This book is about that law: how it came to be, what it was meant to do, how Congress has coped with its massive array of new procedures, how it has altered power relations between Congress and the White House, whether it has affected federal budget policy.

The body of the book is divided into three parts. In the first, the experience of budget reform will be examined in narrative form. One chapter will study how Congress was able to adopt such sweeping new procedures with hardly a vote of opposition. Two others will be devoted to the 1976 fiscal year, when Congress implemented some of the new procedures, and the 1977 fiscal year, when the entire process took effect. The second part will explore the new institutions created by budget reform—the House and Senate Budget Committees in one chapter and the Congressional Budget Office in a second. The third part will analyze the impact of budget reform. Four chapters will concentrate on its influence on spending and tax legislation, the authorizing and appropriating committees, presidential impoundment powers, and presidential domination of budget policy-making.

Judging the success or failure of budget reform is a tricky business. Some members of Congress hoped that it would produce a more conservative fiscal policy—tighter spending and smaller deficits. Others looked for more liberal spending priorities—more spending for domestic programs and less for defense. But all factions would find the following to be legitimate questions to ask about budget reform:

- Did the new process, unlike the 1946 reform, survive?

- Did Congress use it to set fiscal policy—that is, to prepare a budget suitable to economic conditions?

- Did Congress use it to determine the government's spending priorities?

- Could Congress at last enact spending and revenue legislation before the beginning of the new fiscal year?

- Did senators and representatives grow more sophisticated in their understanding of the federal budget?

- Did Congress establish itself as an equal partner with the president in the making of federal budget policy?

If these questions could be answered affirmatively, Congress no longer would be the disorganized collection of 535 men and women who enacted spending and revenue legislation but could not shape it into a coherent expression of budget policy. It finally would have exercised the power that Hamilton had tried to ensure for Congress nearly two centuries earlier—the power over the purse.

CHAPTER 2

ESTABLISHING BUDGET
REFORM

ONE MIGHT SUPPOSE that the 1974 legislation instituting budget reform would have faced awesome and possibly fatal opposition in Congress. After all, it altered many of the familiar patterns by which Congress conducted its business. It established a new timetable for considering all tax and spending legislation, with deadlines that would force committees to act much earlier in the year than was their custom. Most important, it threatened nearly all committees—but especially the Appropriations Committees—with a loss of power to the new Budget Committees.

Yet the legislation sailed through Congress with unanimous support in the Senate and only token opposition in the House. Budget reform's sponsors had imbued their legislation with the image of motherhood and apple pie. It became difficult for members of Congress to oppose "responsible" procedures for writing the federal budget.

At the same time, the sponsors packaged legislation that contained a potential benefit for almost everyone. Ideologues from one end of the political spectrum to the other looked to budget reform to advance their causes. For conservatives, there was the hope that the new budget process would help them hold down federal spending. For liberals, there was a

possibility of shifting spending priorities from defense to domestic programs. Democrats would have a procedure for reducing the power of a Republican president to impound
funds voted by Congress.

Budget reform's authors tried to minimize the threat to
existing centers of congressional power. For committees worried about losing jurisdiction, there was the assurance that the
tasks performed by the Budget Committees would be new
ones—the new committees would not violate the turf of the
old ones. For the Appropriations Committees, which were
especially worried about encroachment by the new Budget
Committees, there were curbs on the use of "backdoor spending," which had stripped those committees of their grip on
total federal spending.

Finally, the procedures established by budget reform were
designed to improve the quality of congressional decision-
making, regardless of a member's political ideology or committee assignments. For all members worried about losing
their power over the purse to the president, the budget process provided an opportunity to assert congressional influence over fiscal policy and spending priorities.

THE 1946 FIASCO

The architects of budget reform in the 1970s had an important model to study, negative though it was. In 1946, Congress demonstrated how *not* to reform its approach to the
federal budget. Congress included budget reform in the massive 1946 Legislative Reorganization Act, which also modified
the jurisdictions of most congressional committees, set out
rules for the size and shape of congressional staffs, required
the registration of lobbyists, and allowed a limited measure of
home rule for the District of Columbia. These provisions, far
closer than the budget to the hearts of most members of
Congress, received most of their attention. By comparison,
budget reform was an afterthought.

According to the provisions of the two-sentence budget reform section, the spending and tax committees of the House and Senate—more than a hundred members altogether—were to meet at the beginning of each year and report a budget resolution by February 15. The resolution was to contain a revenue total and a spending ceiling for a fiscal year that would not even begin for another four and a half months, with no allowance for unforeseen developments that might change the nation's budget needs. There was no mechanism to enforce the totals—nothing to stop Congress from violating its spending ceiling.

From the first, the new budget process became embroiled in partisan wrangling between President Truman and the Republicans, who gained control of Congress in the 1946 elections. In 1947, the members of the Appropriations, Finance, and Ways and Means Committees reported a budget resolution $6 billion below the spending figure Truman had requested in his budget. Rep. George H. Mahon, an Appropriations Committee Democrat, complained that there were no facts to support a $6 billion cut. But Rep. John Taber, the Republican who was Appropriations Committee chairman in 1947, said he had been studying the budget for three months. "We have not drawn these figures out of a hat, but have a good idea of what we are basing them on," Taber claimed.[1]

The House accepted the spending cut on a party-line vote. But in the Senate, a number of Republicans admitted that there was no particular basis for the $6 billion cut. Sen. Eugene D. Millikin, the Republican chairman of the Finance Committee, successfully recommended reducing the cut to $4.5 billion.[2] The House and Senate versions of the resolution were sent to a conference committee of House and Senate members, who were unable to agree on a compromise. The entire year passed without adoption by Congress of a budget resolution. The budget procedure had no perceptible impact on actual federal spending, which turned out to be

BUDGET REFORM—1974 STYLE

During the decades following the failed reform of 1946, the federal budget slipped further and further out of congressional control as "backdoor spending"[8] continued to grow. To be sure, there were myriad proposals for change; for example, Sen. John L. McClellan regularly introduced legislation to establish a Joint Budget Committee to supervise budget policy. But such proposals received scant attention, and the symptoms of an uncontrollable budget grew increasingly apparent. The deteriorating economy of the 1970s underscored the incapacity of Congress to set fiscal policy—that is, to use the budget to help achieve particular economic goals. The deficits—greater than $23 billion in the 1971 and 1972 fiscal years—dramatized Congress's failure to consider how best to spend its limited resources. But these circumstances alone did not threaten the status quo. The irony of budget reform is that a man who was hardly a champion of a strong Congress—Richard Nixon—forced Congress to strengthen itself.

As his first term came to an end in 1972, President Nixon began making unprecedented use of impoundments. In the summer of that year, Nixon challenged Congress to set a ceiling of $250 billion on fiscal 1973 outlays. The fiscal year had already begun, and estimated outlays for the year were about $253 billion. Nixon's proposal put Congress on the spot. If it enacted the ceiling, it would have to make some unpleasant decisions about what programs to cut, or give the president the authority to impound funds as he chose. But if it didn't, Nixon would brand the Democratic Congress as a hotbed of reckless spenders—with the election just months away.

Congress attempted to straddle the issue. It rejected the ceiling, but, to blunt criticism of its inability to control spending, it established a Joint Study Committee on Budget Control. Even then, budget reform had a dual personality; some members of Congress viewed it as a way to reduce spending, others simply as a more efficient method of managing budget decisions. The joint study committee was to review "the procedures which should be adopted by the Congress for the purpose of improving congressional control of budgetary outlay and receipt totals, including procedures for establishing and maintaining an overall view of each year's budgetary outlays which is fully coordinated with an overall view of the anticipated revenues for that year. . . ."[9]

Fiscal conservatives, who led the effort to establish the joint committee, made sure that they controlled it. Congress loaded the committee with representatives of the House Appropriations and Ways and Means Committees and the Senate Appropriations and Finance Committees, whose members were viewed as more fiscally conservative than Congress as a whole. Of the thirty-two joint study committee members, seven came from each of the spending and tax committees, while only four represented the rest of the House and Senate. At its first meeting on January 10, 1973, the joint committee chose as its cochairmen the second-ranking Democrats on the House Appropriations and Ways and Means Committees— Jamie L. Whitten and Al Ullman. It appointed four vice chairmen, three from the Senate and one from the House, two Democrats and two Republicans.[10]

The joint study committee on April 18 proposed a bill[11] that would have clamped tight controls on congressional spending. The new process would be the responsibility of House and Senate Budget Committees, one-third of whose members would come from the Appropriations Committees, one-third from the Ways and Means and Finance Committees, and one-third from the rest of the House and Senate. By May 1 of each year, Congress would adopt a ceiling for spending and the deficit in the fiscal year to begin two months later. Congress would have to enact a tax surcharge if necessary to achieve the required deficit. New "backdoor" spending would cease; from then on, new spending programs would be effective only as provided in appropriations bills. The unanimous vote by the joint study committee for its bill on April 16 reflected not complete accord on every provision, but rather agreement with the goal of congressional budget control.

There was no such consensus in Congress as a whole. Liberals feared that budget control would spell defeat for many of their spending programs. The House Democratic Study Group and the Americans for Democratic Action, liberal groups inside and outside Congress, objected to the predominance of spending and tax committee members on the proposed Budget Committees. They expected that the Budget Committees would be just as fiscally conservative as they perceived the spending and tax committees to be. And they objected vigorously to the setting of a firm spending ceiling by May 1 of every year, before Congress acted on individual spending bills.

SENATE ACTION

In the Senate, one subcommittee and two full committees worked over the joint study committee's budget reform bill before sending it to the Senate floor. Original jurisdiction was with the Government Operations Subcommittee on Budgeting, Management, and Expenditures, where the key issue was the early spending ceiling recommended by the joint study committee. Republican Charles H. Percy led the charge for an early ceiling as the best way to force Congress to control spending. Edmund S. Muskie, a Democrat, pressed for a more flexible target that would guide Congress—but not bind it—as it took up individual spending and tax bills.

Muskie argued that a new budget process would work only if it was neutral—if it didn't help one side or the other in debates over particular issues. But early spending ceilings would inevitably work to the advantage of conservatives who wanted to reduce spending. Liberals would rebel and ultimately sabotage the process. Muskie maintained that targets, in place of ceilings, would provide sufficient pressure on Congress to keep spending under control, because it would be readily apparent to the voters if Congress violated its targets without good reason. Muskie enlisted the support of Republican Bill Brock, a conservative who agreed that the new budget process would need liberal support. But Percy had the backing of fellow Republican William V. Roth and three southern Democrats, and his approach carried the subcommittee by votes of 5 to 4.[12]

On other important issues, the subcommittee took initiatives that eventually became law. Diverging from the joint study committee recommendation, the subcommittee endorsed a Budget Committee whose membership would be drawn from the entire Senate, with no requirement that any members come from the Appropriations and Finance Committees. It also proposed the establishment of a Congressional Office of the Budget to supply Congress with the kind of high-quality budget information that the Office of Management and Budget provided to the president. (The joint study committee had asked merely for a joint staff to serve the two Budget Committees, but the Senate subcommittee wanted a larger and more independent office that could analyze budget policy.) Finally, the subcommittee pushed the beginning of the fiscal year back to October 1, to give Congress three more months to put the federal budget in place before the fiscal year began. (Since 1968, Congress had not enacted a single annual appropriations bill before July 1, the beginning of the fiscal year for which appropriations bills were effective.)

The subcommittee's bill went next to the full Government Operations Committee, where Muskie engineered a compromise over the issue of early spending ceilings. Congress would set a ceiling each spring on total spending, but it would be free to juggle expenditures for individual programs so long as the overall ceiling was not breached. As reported by the Government Operations Committee, the bill aroused nearly unanimous opposition among other Senate committee chairmen. Complaining that the early spending ceilings

would subordinate their roles to that of the new Budget Committee, they succeeded in having the bill referred to the Rules
and Administration Committee for another look. Sen. Robert
C. Byrd, chairman of the Subcommittee on the Standing
Rules of the Senate, took charge. "I wanted to be sure that the
bill would be workable and that it would not too greatly dis-
turb the existing methods of doing business in the Senate,"
Byrd said.[13]

Byrd decided to rewrite the Government Operations bill
entirely, and he named a group of forty-five staff members,
including even a couple from the House Appropriations
Committee, to work out the details. The staff members,
headed by Herbert N. Jasper of the Senate Labor and Public
Welfare Committee, tried to make the bill acceptable to the
entire Senate. For concerned Senate committee chairmen,
they changed the early spending ceiling to a target of the kind
advocated by Muskie. For liberals, they killed the section that
would forbid new entitlement programs—those that guarantee federal benefits for certain kinds of individuals, such as the
disabled and the unemployed. In its place they substituted a
provision to give the Appropriations Committees a chance to
amend new entitlement legislation with provisions limiting
spending authority. They also added a section to prohibit
presidential impoundments designed to reverse congressional policy. (The Senate already had passed such a bill, but
it was a likely target for a veto if it was sent to President Nixon
by itself.)

The effort to attract broad support for budget reform succeeded. On March 22, 1974, the Senate passed the rewritten
version of the bill by a vote of 80 to 0.

HOUSE ACTION

In the House, the Democratic leadership referred the joint
study committee's bill to the Rules Committee. The chairman
and second-ranking Democrat of that committee, wishing not

to become embroiled in such a complicated issue, deferred to Richard Bolling, the Democrat next in seniority. A long-time advocate of budget reform, Bolling worked with John E. Barriere, House Speaker Carl Albert's top staff aide, to turn the joint committee's bill into one that Bolling thought would be workable.

Bolling felt he had to develop a set of procedures that the House could support with near unanimity. He accurately foresaw that when the new procedures took effect it would be almost impossible to develop a congressional budget that would be acceptable to a majority of the House. Actual congressional budgets surely would turn out to be too liberal for some House members and too conservative for others. They would be adopted, Bolling felt, only if they received the votes not only of those who supported the budgets themselves but also of those who supported the budget process.

Bolling quickly replaced the early spending ceilings of the joint study committee's bill with targets much like those in the final version of the Senate-passed bill. He felt congressional committees could not tolerate any process that dictated their spending and tax decisions before they made them. Ullman fought to the end for early ceilings, but the Rules Committee supported Bolling.

Organized labor felt that even the early spending targets would have the effect of making it more difficult for members of Congress to vote for social programs. Labor's concerns were reflected in the persisting skepticism of many House liberals for budget reform. In a move calculated to draw liberal support, Bolling worked to include in the bill a provision allowing Congress to veto any presidential impoundment. First he needed the House to vote for a separate anti-impoundment bill. It did so on July 25, 1973, by a vote of 251 to 164, but only after a motion to recommit the bill to the Rules Committee was defeated by just four votes. Then in the Rules Committee, Bolling attached the impoundment provision—and with it the allegiance of many liberals—to the budget reform bill.

Bolling also sought the support of the House Appropriations Committee, which feared losing jurisdiction—and power—to a Budget Committee. He diligently kept its chairman, George H. Mahon, privy to all maneuverings over the bill. For Mahon, he retained a provision—similar to the proposal of the joint study committee—to stop all new backdoor spending. Finally, Mahon benefited from the budget process deadlines. For years he had complained that the Appropriations Committee was late with its legislation only because the committees in charge of legislation authorizing appropriations were late with theirs. So the Rules Committee version of budget reform included a requirement that all authorizing legislation for the coming fiscal year be enacted by March 31, only three months into each new session of Congress.

Most of Bolling's efforts were in behalf of others, but he also had one pet goal of his own for budget reform. He wanted the new process to focus congressional attention on spending priorities, which always got lost in the shuffle when Congress went through the budget piece by piece. It was his idea to divide the annual spring spending target among the sixteen functions of the federal budget—defense, health, income security, and the like. From the standpoint of writing a budget, it would have made more sense to divide spending instead among the appropriations bills and other spending bills, since that was where Congress made its basic decisions. But Bolling knew other congressional committees would oppose the process if it allowed budget resolutions to dictate the size of their legislation.

Bolling was not alone in shaping the House budget bill. Whitten, a cochairman of the joint study committee, played an important role by developing his own bill, designed to meet some of the criticisms of the joint committee's approach. It was Whitten who proposed that fewer than half of the new

Budget Committee's members come from the Appropriations and Ways and Means Committees, and who suggested that membership on the Budget Committee be rotated to prevent it from becoming a "super-duper committee."[14] He also proposed a fiscal year beginning on November 1, four months later than current practice. The Senate Government Operations subcommittee that had already begun working on legislation persuaded him to change the date to October 1— Congress does hardly any work in October anyway in years in which there are congressional elections in November.

As was the case in the Senate, budget reform's advocates in the House succeeded in building momentum for their cause. When the Rules Committee's bill went to the House floor on December 5, 1973, there was only a smattering of opposition, mostly from liberals Democrats. The vote was 386 to 23.

The conference committee of House and Senate members who reconciled the two versions of the budget reform bill was remarkable for the infrequency of its meetings. Despite the complexity of the issues—or, in a sense, because of it—the conference committee met only twice. At the first session, the only subject was impoundment—an emotional issue on which House and Senate provisions were quite different—and deadlock was quick. House members insisted on a version of their procedure for overturning impoundments opposed by Congress, while senators said the president should not even be allowed to propose impoundments in violation of congressional policy.

Two months later, having met not at all in the interim, the same conferees reached a quick and peaceful accord on the entire budget reform bill. In fact, the impoundment issue was not even discussed. The reason: during the intervening two months, a host of House and Senate staff members met almost daily to write the entire bill. Democrats controlled most of the staff members, and they readily endorsed their product. Rep. Dave Martin, the ranking Republican on the House Rules Committee, complained that the conference committee was little more than a "rubber stamp" for the staff.[15] But despite their grumbling that the new form of budget control would not be strict enough, Republicans went along with the conference bill. The final floor votes were 401 to 6 in the House on June 18, 1974, and 75 to 0 in the Senate on June 21. President Nixon signed the bill into law on July 18, just twenty-one days before Watergate forced him out of office.

BUDGET REFORM'S PROVISIONS

The Congressional Budget and Impoundment Control Act of 1974,[16] as finally signed into law, contained a wealth of complex provisions in its ten titles, fifty-four sections and forty-seven pages. First, it set up three new congressional units:

- *House Budget Committee.* The new committee in the House had twenty-three members—five from the Appropriations Committee, five from the Ways and Means Committee, eleven from other committees, one from the Democratic leadership, and one from the Republican leadership. (Membership was increased to twenty-five in 1975 with the addition of two more at-large members.) It was the House's first rotating committee—no member was allowed to serve for more than four years in any ten.

- *Senate Budget Committee.* The Senate's new committee had fifteen members (increased to sixteen in 1975), chosen, like those of all other committees, by the Democratic and Republican caucuses.

- *Congressional Budget Office.* In addition to the Budget Committees' own staffs, a Congressional Budget Office was established to perform a variety of functions spelled out by the act. It must report annually to Congress on alternative budget strategies for the year ahead. It must regularly compare spending and revenue legislation with the most recent congressional budget resolution. It must study the state of the economy. Its director was to be appointed jointly by the speaker of the House and the president pro tempore of the Senate to a four-year term. The size of the CBO staff was not spelled out by the act.

With the help of its new Budget Committees and the CBO, Congress was to follow a new budget-making timetable:

Action to be completed:	*On or before:*
President submits current services budget to Congress	November 10
President submits annual budget proposals to Congress	Fifteen days after Congress meets
Congressional committees make budget recommendations to Budget Committees	March 15
CBO reports to Budget Committees on alternative budget strategies	April 1
Budget Committees report first budget resolution for coming fiscal year	April 15
Congress adopts first budget resolution	May 15
Congressional committees report all authorizing legislation	May 15
Congress begins floor action on spending and revenue bills	After adoption of first budget resolution

Congress passes all spending and tax bills	Seven days after Labor Day
Congress adopts second budget resolution	September 15
Congress passes budget reconciliation bill	September 25
Fiscal year begins	October 1

The president's current services budget, which begins the budget cycle nearly a year before the fiscal year begins, is an estimate of the cost of maintaining all current programs in the coming fiscal year. It is to be the base against which to measure all proposals for change in the budget. The first formal action by Congress is the submission by March 15 of reports by all committees with jurisdiction over spending or tax legislation. The reports are to tell the Budget Committees what kinds of programs the other committees of Congress would like to put in place in the coming fiscal year.

The congressional budget is to take the form of concurrent resolutions, which require adoption by both the House and the Senate but not presidential signature. The first budget resolution sets targets designed to guide Congress as it proceeds to pass individual spending and tax bills. The Budget Committees prepare the resolution, using the March 15 reports, the president's budget proposals, the CBO report, and the information they develop during their own hearings. The resolution includes five budget totals—outlays, budget authority, revenue, deficit (or surplus), and public debt level. (Budget authority is granted by Congress to authorize the executive branch to spend money immediately or in future fiscal years. Outlays are actual cash transactions.) Outlays and budget authority are divided among the sixteen budget functions. The conference report on the resolution, written jointly

by the House and Senate Budget Committees, allocates outlays and budget authority among congressional committees,
so that they will have targets for total spending in their jurisdiction.

Legislation authorizing spending in subsequent appropriations bills must be reported by committees no later than May
15, although there is no deadline for their enactment. Appropriations and tax bills may not be debated by the full House
or Senate until Congress adopts the first budget resolution,
which sets spending and revenue targets. The same is true of
backdoor spending bills—those that require spending without action in appropriations bills. New backdoor spending
programs that provide executive agencies with authority to
borrow money from the Treasury or enter into contracts are
prohibited; appropriations bills are now necessary to make
such programs effective. Legislation entitling individuals to
federal benefits, if in excess of the first budget resolution,
must be referred to the Appropriations Committees, which
have fifteen days to add provisions limiting spending.

Congress must dispose of all its regular spending and tax
legislation between adoption of the first budget resolution
and a week after Labor Day. Then it must pass a second
resolution that reaffirms the first or revises it in light of changing economic conditions and subsequent congressional action on individual spending and tax bills. The second
resolution is binding; after it is adopted, Congress may not
enact a spending bill that would force spending over the
resolution's total or a tax bill that would cut revenue below
it. Only total budget authority and outlays—not the amounts
for each function—are binding.

It might happen that at the time the second resolution is
adopted, individual spending and revenue bills are already on
a course that would result in violation of the resolution. In
that event, the resolution must direct the relevant congressional committees to prepare legislation bringing spending
and revenue in line. The reconciliation bill, as the resulting

legislation would be called, would have the effect of reversing spending and revenue decisions that Congress had already made. The reconciliation bill is to be enacted by September 25, just six days before the beginning of the new fiscal year —and less than two months before the budget cycle begins for the next fiscal year.

CHAPTER 3

THE FIRST YEAR

WHEN SEN. JOHN C. STENNIS reported the annual military procurement bill to the Senate floor for final approval on August 1, 1975, he understandably expected little trouble. As chairman of the Senate Armed Services Committee, he deservedly enjoyed a reputation as a powerful man. He had fought and won many battles for a strong military. The Senate already had voted 77 to 6 in favor of its version of the procurement bill, which included billions of dollars for the B-1 bomber and many less exceptional engines of war. The new version, a compromise with a bill that had been passed in the House, authorized only $750 million more than the $25 billion that the Senate already had approved. In a $400 billion budget, the difference seemed piddling.

But to Sen. Edmund Muskie, chairman of the Senate Budget Committee, the extra spending threatened the sanctity of the new budget process. According to Muskie's computations, the bill exceeded the defense spending target Congress had included in its first budget resolution, and Muskie determined to make the bill a test case. He sought the support of some Senate Republicans, including Sen. Henry Bellmon, the top-ranking Republican on the Budget Committee. Unlike Muskie, Bellmon regularly supported requests for high defense spending. But in this case, he decided that adherence to the budget resolution was more important than his own views on the issue. The Budget Committee presented a bipartisan front.

And the Budget Committee won; the Senate voted down Stennis's bill by a margin of 48 to 42. The confrontation was a critical one, because it was the first time a congressional budget resolution had been used to try to change legislation on the Senate floor. The amount of money was not significant; in fact, the ultimate resolution with the House left the bill only $250 million below the level that the Senate had rejected. But that didn't really matter. What mattered was that Muskie had used the budget process to challenge one of the most powerful committee chairmen in the Senate—and had won. If Stennis had prevailed, he would have shown Congress that it could safely ignore the dictates of the budget process.

Muskie's victory, largely symbolic rather than substantive, said a lot about the congressional budget process in its first year. On the whole, the Budget Committees in the Senate and the House had a rather slight impact on the shape of legislation turned out by Congress in 1975. But they made the rest of Congress stand up and take notice of the power that was potentially theirs, demonstrating to the Senate and the House that they could make individual pieces of legislation fit into something that had never existed before—a congressional budget.

CHOOSING COMMITTEE MEMBERS

After enactment of the budget reform act in the summer of 1974, Democrats and Republicans in the House and Senate had to choose members of the new Budget Committees. In both chambers, Democrats were chosen who were somewhat more liberal (that is, more favorably disposed toward spending for social purposes and less likely to approve military spending) than congressional Democrats as a whole. Especially in the House, Republicans countered by naming some of their staunchest conservatives to the Budget Committees.

In the Senate, Muskie, one of the chief authors of budget reform, put himself forward as a candidate for chairman of the new committee. No significant opposition developed, and Muskie, two years before the front runner in the race for the Democratic presidential nomination, had built himself a new power base in the Senate. For the other eight Democratic seats, the Democratic Steering Committee chose senators who were diverse in their geography, seniority, and philosophy.

Twenty-seven of the Senate's forty-two Republicans applied for the six Republican seats, and the Republican Conference—all Republicans in the Senate—filled four of them with Republicans who were campaigning for reelection in the fall. When the 94th Congress opened in 1975, five of these six seats on the Budget Committee turned over—one former member had been defeated and four resigned. So when the Budget Committee began its first year of real operations, all but one of its Republicans were new, including Henry Bellmon of Oklahoma, who became the ranking minority member.

In the House, Democrats bypassed their traditional way of naming committee members in favor of a new process that was much more democratic (with a small "d"). They did not allow their Committee on Committees—then controlled by Wilbur D. Mills, chairman of the Ways and Means Committee—to exercise its customary control. Instead, the Democratic Caucus—all House Democrats—delegated to itself the power to elect Democratic Budget Committee members according to the formula that the budget reform act had set for membership on the committee. (There was one exception; House Speaker Carl Albert appointed the party leadership's representative on the committee.) Mills nominated three Ways and Means representatives, Appropriations Committee chairman

Mahon nominated three Democrats from his committee, and the Democratic Steering and Policy Committee nominated seven at-large candidates. Other nominations were allowed by any five Democrats, and three additional Democrats were nominated this way. But the Democratic Caucus elected all the original nominees.

The caucus also retained the right to elect the Budget Committee chairman. Until the week before the caucus was to vote, Brock Adams of Washington, a liberal who had Albert's support, was the only candidate. Then Mills put forward his own choice: Al Ullman, the second-ranking Democrat on Mills's Ways and Means Committee. Ullman defeated Adams by a vote of 113 to 90 and served as Budget Committee chairman for the remainder of 1974. But early in 1975 Ullman became Ways and Means chairman when Mills, tarnished by a liquor and sex scandal, stepped down. The caucus then elected Adams to replace Ullman as Budget Committee chairman.

House Republican leader John J. Rhodes kept to himself most of the power to select the nine Budget Committee Republicans. He accepted the nominations of the Appropriations and Ways and Means Committees for their two representatives each, appointed the four at-large members, and named himself the leadership representative. The slate he had chosen was distinctly conservative. Rhodes made himself the ranking Budget Committee Republican in 1974, but he resigned from the committee the next year and named Delbert L. Latta of Ohio as his replacement.

Budget Committee chairmen intentionally did not form the same kinds of subcommittees that are integral to the operation of most other congressional committees. They feared that if subcommittees specialized in particular areas of the budget, the committees' work would become as fragmented as the traditional congressional approach to the budget. Instead, task forces were formed in both Budget Committees to develop expertise—but not policy—in defense spending, tax expenditures, and other areas of the budget. But without power to help shape budget resolutions, the task forces wielded little influence.

In addition to the Budget Committees, the budget reform act also mandated the creation of the Congressional Budget Office. The CBO director was to be appointed by the speaker of the House (Carl Albert) and the president pro tempore of the Senate (James O. Eastland), but in practice Albert and Eastland relied on the advice of the Budget Committee chairmen. After months of deadlock, Muskie finally prevailed with his choice of Alice M. Rivlin of the Brookings Institution. But she was not appointed until February 24, 1975—too late for her to put together a CBO staff that could be of much help to Congress until 1976.

PARTIAL IMPLEMENTATION

In their first year, the budget reform act required the Budget Committees to do little more than get ready for 1976. Only then would the procedures spelled out in the act become binding on Congress. But in fact, 1975 turned out to be a more significant year for the new process than had been anticipated. As the Budget Committees organized, the worst recession since World War II gripped the country, accompanied by double-digit inflation. A few committee members feared that the state of the economy might instantly sabotage the new budget procedures. Rep. Robert L. Leggett, a Democrat on the House committee, said Republicans and Democrats were polarized on economic issues and might not be able to agree on a budget policy for Congress to follow. "What will it do to our credibility," he wondered, "if we make substantial errors our first time around?"[1]

But the committee chairmen felt otherwise. Searching for ways to counter the economic policies of the Republican president, congressional Democrats found a handy tool in the new budget process. "With the state of the economy as it is, it isn't an option to go right to work, it's a command," said Ullman shortly after being elected the House Budget Committee's first chairman.[2] Likewise, Muskie and Adams, who replaced Ullman as chairman early in 1975, refused to sit on their hands for twelve months. The failing economy, said Muskie, meant that budget reform "assumes an even larger role than was originally contemplated when it was enacted scarcely eight months ago."[3]

The staffs of the House and Senate Budget Committees recognized that the full range of new budget procedures probably was more than the committees could handle in their first year. The committee staffs were just taking shape, and the Congressional Budget Office did not even exist until February of 1975. Staff aides felt it would be impossible to do all the budgetary computations that would be necessary to implement all the new procedures. And they thought it would be too much to ask Congress, still unfamiliar with the procedures, to meet all the difficult deadlines that would be mandatory in the next year. So the Budget Committee staffs proposed a plan for implementing some of the new procedures, and the Budget Committees embraced their limited approach.

Under the plan, the committees would prepare fiscal 1976 budget resolutions lacking some of the detail that would be required in future years. By specifying congressional targets for spending and revenue, the resolutions would give Congress opportunities to debate the size of the deficit. But only the Budget Committee reports explaining the resolutions— not the resolutions themselves—would divide spending among the sixteen budget functions. The reports would not allocate spending among the various congressional committees with jurisdiction over spending legislation, as they would in the future.

While the two budget resolutions would be less complete than those that followed, they would have the same legal force. The numbers in the first resolution would be targets to guide Congress as it enacted individual spending and revenue bills. The second resolution would set a spending ceiling and a revenue floor that Congress could not violate—without first revising the resolution. The force of the budget resolutions was a point that was lost on some members of Congress, particularly House Republicans, who sneered that the first year of budget reform could have no impact on other congressional action. "Everybody knows it's just a trial run," said Latta.[4] This attitude allowed House Republicans to vote so overwhelmingly against the fiscal 1976 budget resolutions that they nearly wrecked the new process. In the Senate, meanwhile, Stennis and his Armed Services Committee found out just how real budget reform was in its first year.

WRITING A RESOLUTION

The budget reform act set May 15 as the deadline for adoption of the first budget resolution. Congress beat that deadline by one day in its first attempt—but only after some close calls and dramatic turnabouts.

The first step was the duty not of the Budget Committees but of nearly all other congressional committees. The other committees were required to report to the Budget Committees by March 15 on their estimates of the costs of programs under their jurisdiction for the next year. All the committees responded, although some missed the deadline and others provided very sketchy information. Like executive departments and agencies submitting their spending requests to the Office of Management and Budget, most committees asked for more spending authority than they thought they could get. Spending requests in the Senate totaled $60 billion more than President Ford's proposed budget. This allowed Budget Committee members, even the most liberal ones, to claim the role of budget cutter. It also made the other committees suspicious of the Budget Committees' power to overturn their plans for spending legislation. "There's a reasonable amount

of worry among the other committees that we're going to
usurp some of their domain," said Sidney L. Brown, the senior counsel on the Senate Budget Committee's staff.[5]

Budget Committee members tried to neutralize such hos-
tility. Adams opened House Budget Committee markup of
the first budget resolution—the series of meetings at which
the committee prepared a resolution—by recommending that
the committee simply forecast the spending and revenue legislation that Congress was likely to adopt during the coming
months. He did not want to appear to be telling other House
committees what kind of legislation they should prepare. "I
tried to avoid having this committee this year run into a head-
to-head argument with other committees of the House," he
explained.[6]

That approach touched off the first important procedural
argument in the House committee. "If this committee is
merely going to add up numbers, we might as well dissolve,"
Latta complained. He was joined by Rep. Butler Derrick, a
Democrat, who said, "One of these days, this committee is
going to have to make some hard decisions to justify its existence."[7]

Adams agreed, but he said that day should wait until the
next year. For the most part, the committee accepted his
approach; consequently, the budget process had little impact
on spending and revenue legislation in the House in its first
year. Nevertheless, committee members did not hesitate to
argue the pros and cons of individual spending programs.
Occasionally the more activist members succeeded in placing
items in the resolution that Adams felt were unlikely to gain
congressional support—for example, a 5-percent cap on federal pay raises. (As it happened, Congress ultimately approved such a cap after all.)

Committee members examined the budget in great detail.
Like the Post Office and Civil Service Committee, they debated the relative merits of different kinds of retirement programs for federal employees. Like the Armed Services

Committee, they looked at the value of the B-1 bomber. Democrats dominated the debate; an important vote on an extra $3 billion for public works projects was taken when twelve Democrats but no Republicans were present. Committee members found themselves torn between their new duties and their old. As members of the Budget Committee, they were supposed to look at individual spending and revenue decisions in the context of the whole budget. But as members of other committees as well, they continued to champion programs under the jurisdiction of their other committees. Rep. James G. O'Hara, for example, became something of a Budget Committee spokesman for education programs.

After seven days and two nights of laboring through the budget, the House committee found to its surprise that a majority of its members opposed the document that it had drafted. All eight Republicans and three southern Democrats opposed the deficit ($73.2 billion) as too big, and they were joined by two northern Democrats, O'Hara and Elizabeth Holtzman, who felt there was too much money for defense and not enough for the poor. The Democrats who favored the resolution were outvoted 13 to 10.

The stalemate represented the one instance when House Democrats could not singlehandedly keep the budget process moving. Two Republicans came to the rescue. Elford A. Cederberg and Barber B. Conable, Jr., switched their votes, explaining that they felt the full House should have a chance to vote the budget resolution up or down on the House floor. Thus did budget reform survive one of its closest brushes with extinction.

Adams and his Budget Committee had another close call on the House floor. Some Democratic liberals, reacting against Budget Committee restrictions on their favorite programs, voted no. So did all but three Republicans. The resolution was adopted by a vote of 200 to 196, but only after Rep. Thomas P. O'Neill, Jr., the House Democratic leader, amended it to include more domestic spending and make it palatable to some of the disaffected liberals. A defeat would have sent the resolution back to the Budget Committee for changes to make it acceptable to a majority of the House, but Adams contended there was no way to modify it to make it more popular. Spending cuts would have attracted some conservative support at the expense of liberal backing, while spending increases would have had the opposite effect. Either way, Adams felt, changes would have created more opponents than supporters. As Adams discovered, formulating a budget that could be supported by a majority of the House was a chancy process.[8]

Events followed a very different course in the Senate. Unlike Adams, Muskie opened Budget Committee deliberations without a package of budget recommendations of his own. Instead of simply forecasting likely congressional action on spending and revenue bills, Muskie and other committee members consciously tried to write a budget that would attack recession and inflation. At the same time, Senate committee members explored the budget in much less programmatic detail than their House counterparts. Muskie warned them that such excursions would appear to constitute invasions of other committees' domains.

Although Muskie made no comprehensive recommendation for the resolution, he pressed for a number of pieces of the budget, including a $12.4 billion package of programs designed to stimulate the economy. Republicans and southern Democrats trimmed the proposal to $4.5 billion and came within one vote of eliminating it. The committee then voted 8 to 2 to send the resolution it had prepared to the Senate floor.

Muskie faced an uncomfortable choice. Should he oppose the resolution, thus risking its defeat and the ruin of the budget process? Or should he support the resolution, even though he felt it should provide more economic stimulus? Muskie decided to accept the verdict of his committee. "It seemed to me at that point terribly important to establish the credibility of the process," he explained.[9]

Bellmon confronted a comparable dilemma. House Republicans had been unable to support the $73.2 billion deficit that was contained in the House version of the budget resolution. Was the somewhat smaller $67.2 billion deficit in the Senate version something that Bellmon could swallow? He decided it was, because his brief experience with budget policy had convinced him that a sizable deficit was an inevitable by-product of recession. If Muskie was able to support a resolution not exactly suited to his own economic preferences, so was Bellmon. "There's a certain discipline that goes with being on the Budget Committee," he told the Senate. "You can't go to the floor and do your own thing."[10] With Muskie and Bellmon united, the Senate voted 69 to 22 in favor of its version of the budget resolution.

A House-Senate conference committee, comprising members of the two Budget Committees, reconciled the differences between the two versions of the resolution without much difficulty. The stickiest issue was procedural; senators objected that the House had prepared a resolution in which the detail reached down to millions of dollars. The senators felt all numbers should be rounded off to tenths of billions, and anything smaller than $50 million was too small to be considered. Otherwise, according to the Senate argument, other committees would begin complaining that the Budget Committee was telling them exactly how every dollar should be spent. Muskie told the conference, "We've all seen the potential for great strain between the Budget Committee and the policy committees, and we've tried to avoid trespassing on their domain."[11] The conference committee decided to round off all numbers to tenths of billions and to address specific spending programs only when those programs had been the subjects of House floor votes.

The conference committee produced a budget resolution with a total spending target of $367 billion, compared with the $349.4 billion that had been recommended by President Ford. That left the deficit at $68.8 billion, far greater than

Ford's proposed $51.9 billion. The Senate adopted the conference committee version of the budget resolution easily, by voice vote. After hearing House Speaker Carl Albert urge them to "keep the process going," House members voted 230 to 193 for the resolution. For the first time ever, Congress had adopted a strategy for spending the country's money.

ENFORCING THE RESOLUTION

Now the question was this: would Congress be guided by its budget resolution? Or would it, as Latta predicted, continue its old habit of approving individual spending bills without considering the total impact on the budget?[12] Although many members of Congress were not aware of it, the first budget resolution for fiscal 1976 had exactly as much power as first resolutions would have in the future. It was not binding on subsequent congressional action—no first resolution is. Its only power was the power of persuasion. If Congress enacted a spending bill for considerably more money—or considerably less—than the resolution's target, it would do so only with the realization that the public would know that the spending guideline had been abandoned. A close vote might be determined by the argument that a particular program did or did not conform to the budget resolution.

Adams and Muskie took to the House and Senate floors regularly when spending bills were being debated to notify their colleagues about the relation between the bills and the budget resolution. More often than not, they said the bills were within the resolution's targets; on most other occasions they said the bills exceeded the targets by so little that they would raise no objections. Rare were the times when other House or Senate committees sought approval of legislation that flagrantly violated the targets.

When Adams found out that other House committees were preparing legislation outside the targets, he tried to divert them without a public confrontation. For example, he told the

Post Office and Civil Service Committee that one of its bills, which would have allowed federal employees to retire earlier with full pension benefits, was too costly. The bill, the target of opposition from a variety of quarters, never was called to a vote.[13] Adams's staff worked hard to discover bills in violation of the targets before the bills were sent to the House floor. On the rare occasions when it failed, Adams sometimes made his opposition public, as in the case of an unsuccessful bill to reorganize the Postal Service.[14]

In the Senate, meanwhile, Muskie did not hesitate to go public. During preparation by the Budget Committee of the resolution, Muskie had cautioned against approval or disapproval of particular programs for fear of offending the committees with jurisdiction over them. But that sensitivity began to evaporate as the year wore on, and Muskie showed no reluctance to oppose individual pieces of legislation turned out by those committees. He wanted to put his Budget Committee on the map.

The most celebrated case was the victory by Muskie and the Budget Committee in the struggle over the military procurement bill. At the same time, to prove they were not discriminating against a single category of spending, Muskie and Bellmon pushed the Senate to vote, 76 to 0, to make cuts in a school lunch bill already approved by a House-Senate conference committee. Muskie also used budget arguments to explain his vote in favor of a 5-percent pay raise for federal employees—including members of Congress—instead of the 8.66 percent that cost-of-living calculations would have allowed. Adams voted against the 5-percent limit, but it was accepted anyway.

If the targets of the first budget resolution are to set spending priorities, Congress must make sure not only that spending in each category of federal activity stays within the target, but also that it does not fall far short of the target. But only once during a debate over particular programs did the Budget Committees take the side of more spending. The issue was education; Ford had vetoed the education appropriations bill because it exceeded his budget request. But Muskie and Adams pointed out that the bill was within the budget resolution's targets for education, and they told Congress it would be selling education short if it accepted Ford's veto. Both the House and the Senate voted overwhelmingly to override the veto.

THE SECOND RESOLUTION

For a variety of reasons, the second budget resolution that year did not work the way it was supposed to in the future. Under the budget reform act, Congress is to adopt the second resolution by September 15, two weeks before the beginning of the new fiscal year. But the first time around, Congress did not take final action on the second resolution until December 12—nearly three months late.

The Budget Committees felt no need to rush to meet the deadline. For one thing, the 1976 fiscal year had begun on July 1; the switch to October 1 would not occur until the next year. So the committees knew there was no way to adopt the second resolution before the fiscal year began. Besides, the second resolution is not supposed to be adopted until Congress has completed work on all regular spending and revenue legislation for the coming year. But in September 1975, Congress had yet to act on most of the big fiscal 1976 spending bills. In future years, congressional committees with jurisdiction over spending bills—most notably the two Appropriations Committees—would be required to work at a frantic pace early each year to get their legislation to the White House by early September. But in the first year with the new procedures, the Budget Committees did not try to force the Appropriations Committees to adhere to the new timetable. As the dates for enactment of spending legislation slipped further and further behind, so did the date for adopting the second budget resolution. Finally the Budget Committees moved the resolution through Congress shortly before it adjourned for the year. That meant that the 1976 fiscal year, which had begun on July 1, was nearly half over before Congress adopted the second budget resolution for that year. It was too late for Congress to do much to change the course of federal spending and revenue for that year. So the Budget Committees made no effort in the second resolution to alter substantially the budgetary decisions that Congress already had made.

The second resolution can revise the spending and revenue targets of the first if Congress finds that changing economic conditions dictate a new fiscal policy. In 1975, the Budget Committees determined that the targets of the first resolution were still appropriate. That was another reason for not touching already enacted spending and revenue bills, which for the most part met the targets of the first resolution. In addition, the Budget Committees were reluctant to try to force a strong second resolution down the throat of Congress in their first year. They were still trying to have Congress accept them as legitimate, and they didn't want to antagonize friends by trying to make Congress change decisions it had already made.

Not that they didn't have opponents. They did—including some of their own members. Holtzman said, "While I know the limitations faced by the Budget Committee because of its short existence and the magnitude and complexity of its task, I believe it has nonetheless failed to use opportunities that were available to effect a significant change in national priorities."[15] Latta characterized the budget process as "just adding up a lot of figures."[16] The fact that it was the Holtzmans and the Lattas—the most liberal and most conservative House members—who wanted a more forceful budget process underlined the difficulty of becoming more aggressive. Holtzman would have used the process to cut defense spending and invigorate domestic programs; Latta would have reduced the deficit by cutting domestic programs. There was no way that the Budget Committees could have gained majority support for either approach.

The committee deliberations on the second resolution were consistent with the tone that had been set during consideration of the first. In the spring, the committees largely had predicted what Congress would do with spending and revenue legislation; now they incorporated the outcome of congressional action into the second resolution. The version of the resolution passed by the House Budget Committee was taken almost entirely from Adams's recommendations, which were patterned on congressional action to date. On the House floor, the Democratic leadership amended the resolution to include slightly more money to pay for jobs programs and to meet the costs of the accord between Israel and Egypt that Secretary of State Henry A. Kissinger had just helped negotiate. The House then passed the resolution by a vote of 225 to 191, a landslide compared with the four-vote margin in the spring.

In the Senate, Muskie followed his pattern of presenting his committee with no recommendation for the resolution. Instead, he notified the committee of the status of spending and revenue legislation to date, and suggested that the committee use that as a basis for the second resolution. At one point Muskie deviated from this approach, when he proposed a defense spending level $600 million below that of the military appropriations bill that the Appropriations Committee recently had sent to the Senate floor. Democrat Ernest F. Hollings said it would be stupid for the Budget Committee to pick a fight with the Appropriations Committee over a "stinking $600 million," and Muskie's proposal lost, 9 to 6.[17] Once again Muskie was defeated in committee, and once again he defended his committee's resolution on the Senate floor. With bipartisan support, the resolution was adopted, 69 to 23.

The usual conference committee of House and Senate Budget Committee members appointed to reconcile the differing versions of the budget resolutions spent little time debating fiscal policy or spending priorities. Among the more time-consuming issues was one over which Congress had no control—the amount of revenue that the government was likely to realize from the sale of offshore oil leases. Senate conferees ultimately agreed to let the resolution reflect more offshore oil income than they felt was probable, and the extra revenue was used to offset the cost of additional education and jobs programs that House conferees insisted upon.

As usual, the Senate handily approved the final version of the budget resolution, this time by a vote of 74 to 19. The House Democratic leadership made the mistake of scheduling the vote on the resolution for a Friday, when many of the resolution's supporters were home in their districts. The error almost proved costly, but the resolution squeaked through the House on a vote of 189 to 187.

A "SUCCESSFUL OPERATION"

The Budget Committees would have been hard pressed if, in their first year, congressional support had built for a spending bill that would have violated the second resolution. A single member of Congress could have blocked such a bill simply by lodging a point of order against it on the House or Senate floor. If they thought the bill worthy of enactment, the Budget Committees would have been forced to report a third budget resolution increasing the spending ceilings of the second. A third resolution is a legitimate tool to make room for increased estimates of the costs of ongoing programs or for spending to meet emergencies not foreseen when the second resolution was adopted. But it also would leave a Democratic Congress open to charges by a Republican president that it was busting its own budget.

Of course, the Budget Committees had been trying to avoid just that kind of predicament when they wrote a second resolution that took into account all spending that Congress had enacted or seemed likely to enact. But after the second resolution, some emergency spending came along in the form of federal aid to keep New York City from going bankrupt. In legislation enacted on December 18, Congress provided $2.3 billion in short-term loans to New York. Enactment of the New York City appropriation did not violate the budget resolution, because Congress at that point had not passed all the other spending legislation that had been anticipated by the resolution. But it used up some of the margin that the Budget Committees had set aside for the supplemental, all-purpose appropriations bill that Congress passes every spring.

Fortunately for the Budget Committees, there was enough spending margin left even after New York City so that Congress never had to worry about breaking the ceiling. The economy was recovering from recession in late 1975 and early 1976, and that meant less spending than had been expected for programs such as unemployment compensation and welfare. The reductions from expected spending levels—which Congress had nothing to do with—were much greater than the $2.3 billion that Congress had authorized for New York City. The recovering economy saved Congress from a confrontation with its own budget ceilings.

When the 1976 fiscal year ended on June 30, spending turned out to fall $8.4 billion below the $374.9 billion ceiling of the second budget resolution. The deficit was $66.5 billion, well below the $74.1 billion limit. The administration, which felt the spending and deficit figures were too high in the second resolution, was unimpressed. "For Congress to congratulate itself on keeping spending within the ceilings they had set in their budget resolutions is about as ridiculous as a high jumper crowing about getting over a bar set at two feet," said OMB Director James T. Lynn.[18]

But to Muskie, the figures proved that the new budget process had worked. "For the fiscal year just ended," he said, "Congress designed a comprehensive budget plan—to end the recession without triggering a new round of inflation. More importantly, we carried the plan to realization. In so doing, Congress exercised a degree of fiscal discipline which in my eighteen years in the Senate is unprecedented."

"The successful operation of this new budget process," Adams added, "is historic not just because of the fiscal responsibility shown, but also because it marks the completion of an economic policy that is distinctly that of the Congress —not the president. It shows that Congress has recaptured from the executive its constitutional role in controlling the power of the purse."[19]

CHAPTER 4

THE SECOND YEAR

BROCK ADAMS HAD ONE overriding goal for the second year
of budget reform: survival. From the day he took over as
chairman of the House Budget Committee, Adams thought
the budget process could easily die in the House. His fears
grew when two budget resolutions squeaked through by mar-
gins of four votes and two votes in 1975. Early in 1976, Adams
carefully cultivated the chairmen of other House committees
—especially Mahon of Appropriations—and asked how the
Budget Committee could help them. He regularly quizzed his
own staff or that of the Congressional Budget Office about
impending threats to the budget process.

There were times when Adams felt uncomfortable in his
role as protector of the new process. When the House debated the first budget resolution for fiscal 1977, his discom-
fort increased as some of the House's most outspoken liberals
condemned the Budget Committee for smothering programs
to benefit the poor. Adams, a liberal himself, turned to a staff
aide sitting beside him on the House floor and whispered,
"What am I doing down here? I ought to be up there with
them." But he knew that following his liberal instincts could
lead only to grief, because the budget resolution would grow
so large that it would lose essential support from moderate
Democrats. At most, he figured, the resolution would be
adopted by ten or fifteen votes.

As it turned out, Adams was wrong. His careful campaign to build support for the budget process succeeded beyond his wildest expectations; the resolution passed by 221 to 155, a margin of 66 votes. Adams picked up new votes from Democrats of all stripes—northern and southern, liberal and conservative, white and black. None of the Budget Committee's Republicans could bring themselves to vote for the resolution, but whereas three Republicans had supported the first resolution on the House floor a year before, thirteen of them did so this time. Adopting a stance much like that of many Republicans in the Senate, these Republicans decided that backing the budget process was more important than opposing the budget's contents. To be sure, this group of Republicans included party liberals who could more easily rationalize the resolution's $52.4 billion deficit. One of them was Margaret M. Heckler, and she explained her vote this way: "Although I believe the total cost of the resolution was too high, I voted for it to express my support for the fiscal discipline that the process represents."[1]

The House vote marked a turning point for the congressional budget process. It meant that the Budget Committee and its chairman could begin to throw their weight around— to try to influence the shape of spending and tax legislation —without fear that the House would respond by defeating a budget resolution and wrecking the new process. "The vote certainly indicates to me," Adams said, "that there is strong overall support for the process."[2]

If caution paid off for Adams, aggressiveness almost doomed Muskie. Buoyed by his successful confrontation with Stennis the previous year, Muskie decided in 1976 to wrestle with one of the most powerful senators, and certainly the best strategist—Finance Committee chairman Russell Long. Some of the Senate's most ardent tax reformers, including Ernest F. Hollings, Edward M. Kennedy, and Gaylord Nelson, enlisted Muskie in their cause early in the year. The first budget resolution, as Muskie steered it through the Senate Budget

Committee in March, included $2 billion in revenue to be raised by eliminating tax expenditures—or, as the tax reformers called them, tax loopholes.

This did not sit well with Long, who had always resented other senators' meddling with his committee's business. He appeared personally at a Budget Committee meeting—something no committee chairman had ever done before—to plead his case. His argument followed two lines. First, he said tax reform legislation rarely raises any revenue in the year in which it takes effect; usually its major provisions take several years to become fully effective. His second argument concerned the nature of the new budget process. The budget resolution, he maintained, should merely identify a target for total federal revenue for the coming fiscal year. It is the job of the Finance Committee, not the Budget Committee, to determine how to reach that total. "You tell us how much money you need, and we'll raise it," Long told the Budget Committee.[3]

Muskie's response showed how much he and Adams differed in their approach to Budget Committee leadership. Muskie told Long that his committee's job was to recommend broad tax and spending policy, not just to predict what committees such as Long's would do. While conceding that the Budget Committee has no business spelling out the details of tax legislation, Muskie said it was perfectly within the committee's jurisdiction to make recommendations on such broad issues as the size of a tax cut and the magnitude of tax reform. "We've got to make some guesses and some *judgments* [emphasis added] as to what ought to be enacted and what will be enacted," he told the Finance Committee chairman.[4]

Long's appeal to the Budget Committee proved fruitless. The committee held to its $2 billion in tax reform—a figure that appeared, under the terms of the budget reform act, not in the resolution itself but in the Budget Committee's accompanying report.[5] The $2 billion remained in the budget resolution that Congress finally adopted on May 13, and it set the

stage for the most bitter dispute to date between a Budget
Committee and another congressional committee. Long won
vote after vote on the Senate floor, but he lost much of what
he had gained when he took the tax bill to conference committee with the House. In the end, Muskie could claim that the
budget process forced Congress to take a look—albeit a
rather hasty one—at the need to reform the tax code.

THE PRELIMINARIES

The budget reform act required the Budget Committees to
put the entire new budget process into effect in 1976 for the
fiscal 1977 budget. The committees had tested most of the
new procedures the previous year, but they saved some of the
most difficult for 1976. For the first time, the coming fiscal
year would not begin until October 1, three months later than
in the past, and Congress would try to enact all its spending
and revenue legislation before then. That meant committees
responsible for legislation that authorized spending for the
coming fiscal year would have to prepare for House or Senate
floor debate by May 15. The Appropriations Committees
would have to compress their enormous workload into less
time. In addition to the new deadlines, the process imposed
additional technical requirements. The Budget Committees
would have to translate the first budget resolution, which
divides spending among the sixteen budget functions, into
the amount of spending under the jurisdiction of each of the
other congressional committees. It was hoped that this exercise, known in budget jargon as a "crosswalk," would make
it easier for congressional committees to understand what the
budget resolution expected of them.

Fiscal 1977 was the first year for which the Office of Management and Budget prepared a current services budget in
November to show the cost of maintaining all current government services in the fiscal year that would begin the following
October. Budget reform's authors had hoped that the current

services budget would be a handy analytical tool, free of political judgments, that could be used to measure proposed changes in the budget. But in fact, OMB had to make a great many judgments as it prepared the fiscal 1977 current services budget. It had to predict economic conditions two years into the future to estimate the costs of such programs as unemployment compensation. It decided to adjust spending for inflation only in the case of programs that had cost-of-living escalators built into law, even though inflation surely would increase the costs of other programs as well. It had to use fiscal 1975 data to define the current costs of operating all of the biggest federal departments, because Congress had not yet enacted any of the major fiscal 1976 appropriations bills. When the Budget Committees prepared the first fiscal 1977 budget resolution in the spring of 1977, they found OMB's November current services estimates dated and inaccurate. The current services budget proved little more than a time-consuming nuisance for OMB.

On Capitol Hill, the second year of budget reform began with the reports from other congressional committees to the Budget Committees on March 15. As one indication that the budget process was catching on, all committees actually complied with the deadline. Most of them simply ratified reports prepared by their staffs, although two of the most important —Senate Finance and House Ways and Means—met for four and three days respectively to review their legislative agendas item by item. Complaints were common that it was too early in the year for the committees to know what legislation they would report. "We haven't the faintest idea what we're talking about," said Congressman Conable during a Ways and Means meeting.[6]

The budget reform act says little about what the March 15 reports must include. The Budget Committees made recommendations, but the other committees produced a variety of interpretations. The Senate Armed Services Committee filed the briefest report—a two-page narrative recommending that

Congress not cut from President Ford's requests for spending increases for the military. At the other extreme, the Senate Interior and Insular Affairs Committee submitted a 102-page report that went into great detail, all the way to $2 million for Colorado River salinity control. The two Appropriations Committees steered a middle course, dividing their spending recommendations by budget function and detailing some of the major changes from the President's budget request.

As a rule, the committees tried to include all possible spending programs in their reports lest the excluded programs be frozen out of the congressional budget. Chairman Russell Long recommended to his Senate Finance Committee members, "If one thing closes an option and another leaves it open, I think we ought to leave it open."[7] Two Republicans, Bob Packwood and William V. Roth, complained that the Finance Committee was missing a chance to set spending priorities. "That's why we have the Budget Committee," Long replied.[8]

In the House, Rep. Joe D. Waggoner, Jr., of the Ways and Means Committee supported $150 million for start-up costs for national health insurance even though he opposed the program, because "I do not want to tie the hands of this committee or Congress."[9] The Education and Labor Committee carried this approach to an extreme. President Ford requested $18.5 billion in outlays for programs under the Education and Labor Committee's jurisdiction, and the committee increased that sum by $7.6 billion. Committee Republicans complained that the figures would be useless to the Budget Committee. "We believe," they said, "that one of the most important principles in the new budget process is the requirement that Congress begin making some of the critical decisions about spending priorities."[10]

It is impossible to determine total congressional spending plans simply by adding up all the committees' March 15 reports in the House and the Senate. Some programs were reported twice in each chamber, by the authorizing committee and the appropriating committee. In some cases, competing committees put in bids for jurisdiction over the same program. The House Budget Committee staff tried to compensate for these factors when it determined that if Congress enacted every spending program recommended by at least one House committee, total spending in fiscal 1977 would reach $442 billion, $48 billion more than the president had requested. This high total reflected the care with which committees included in their reports nearly every spending program that had a chance of enactment. In the end, when total spending in the first budget resolution was only $413.3 billion, none of the committees complained that the resolution was squeezing them too hard.

March 15 was also the date when the Congressional Budget Office presented the Budget Committees with its first annual report on budget options for the coming fiscal year. The budget reform act requires the report by April 1, but CBO director Alice Rivlin decided April 1 was too late to have much impact on the first budget resolution. In fact, CBO tried to publish the report several weeks before March 15, but it missed its first deadline when it revised the report in response to Budget Committee criticism of a preliminary version. Even the revised, 393-page report proved of little or no value to the Budget Committees. The report analyzed three budget strategies—a continuation of current policy, the more restrictive economic policy recommended by President Ford, and a more expansionary approach. The Budget Committees found the report too general to help them make decisions on specific budget issues, and they instead relied largely on the March 15 reports of other committees.

THE FIRST RESOLUTION

The Budget Committees broke no new ground in their preparation of the first budget resolution for fiscal 1977. In the House, Adams again presented his proposal for the first budget resolution, and once again it included increases over the president's budget request for domestic programs and cuts in his defense request. Although Adams's defense proposal included substantial growth over the previous fiscal year, the committee increased it still more, nearly to the level that Ford had sought. Majority leader O'Neill, who the previous year had amended budget resolutions on the House floor to make them more suitable to liberals, this year took that action as a member of the Budget Committee. By a vote of 13 to 12, the committee accepted O'Neill's proposal to add money for jobs programs, national health insurance, and federally guaranteed full employment.

If lobbyists had virtually ignored the Budget Committees in 1975, they turned out in force in 1976. Early in the markup, the House committee accepted Latta's amendment to delete $307 million for federal subsidies for second, third, and fourth-class mail. That action brought what Latta called the heaviest two-day lobbying effort he had ever seen from all the groups that benefit from the subsidized rates for lower-class mail. On the last day of committee meetings, Democrat Robert N. Giaimo successfully moved to restore the $307 million. When the committee's vote was complete, a delegation of satisfied lobbyists stood up and left the committee room. One of them, from the Magazine Publishers Association of America, looked in Giaimo's direction and said, "Thank you."[11]

During House Budget Committee markup, James T. Lynn, director of the president's Office of Management and Budget, led a contingent of top OMB officials who sat on the Republican side of the committee room and provided a steady stream of information and advice to the Republican committee members. Lynn's own position was clear. After Adams had recommended a budget resolution that rejected Ford's proposals for tax cuts coupled with spending cuts, Lynn said, "I find the general thrust of chairman Adams's recommendations appalling."[12] Under the watchful eye of the OMB delegation, House Budget Committee Republicans held steadfastly together—

against Adams's recommendations. A year earlier, two Republicans had rescued Adams when he could not win the votes of more extreme Democratic liberals and conservatives on the Budget Committee. But this year, Adams had to get the necessary votes from his own party—and he did. The committee voted 14 to 10 to report the resolution to the House floor.

Adams proceeded to his landmark victory on the House floor. First he had to repel an amendment proposed by Rep. Omar Burleson, a Texas Democrat, to delete the $100 million for start-up costs for two favorite programs of the liberal Democrats—national health insurance and full employment legislation. The amount of money was small, but Adams feared he would lose a lot of liberal votes if these two programs were shut out of the 1977 budget. Burleson's amendment was defeated handily, by a vote of 230 to 153 (although, as it turned out, Congress enacted neither national health insurance nor full employment legislation). In fact, only two floor amendments, both increasing veterans' benefits, succeeded. In the end, the vote of 221 to 155 in favor of the budget resolution was the most satisfying victory of Adams's two years as Budget Committee chairman.[13]

In the Senate Budget Committee, preparations of the first resolution was unexceptional until Long's appearance. As usual, Muskie did not present a package of his own recommendations; instead, the committee worked from the Congressional Budget Office's estimate of the cost of current policies and from the recommendations of other Senate committees on March 15. On the spending side of the budget, Muskie kept a low profile, and the committee produced a budget similar to the House Budget Committee's version. But on the revenue side, Muskie insisted on adding $2 billion through tax reform, and his committee supported him over Long's objections.

For the Senate, budget resolutions already were routine business, and this one was adopted by a vote of 62 to 22. But the Senate's routine choked off any opportunity that the budget resolution might provide for the full Senate to debate spending priorities. When Sen. Alan Cranston proposed an amendment to increase spending for veterans' benefits, majority leader Mike Mansfield, majority whip Robert C. Byrd, and minority whip Robert P. Griffin argued that a vote for Cranston's amendment was a vote against the budget process. "I do not intend to vote for any amendment no matter how meritorious or how nice it is . . ." Mansfield said. Byrd added, " . . . we have got to stand behind the manager of this resolution [Muskie] if we intend to make the budget reform act work." Cranston pleaded for a little flexibility:

> We are talking here about a matter of priorities in spending and, certainly, the Senate as a whole has the right and the obligation to consider what priorities should be high, what should be low and what adjustments should be made in what the Budget Committee recommends to us.[14]

But Cranston's amendment never even came to a vote. On a motion by Muskie, the Senate voted, 53 to 21, to table his amendment.

The conference committee of House and Senate Budget Committee members appointed to reconcile the two versions of the budget resolution was quite unremarkable. As in 1975, the most difficult issue was whether to state spending and revenue totals to the nearest million dollars, as the House wanted, or to round off to tenths of billions, as the Senate insisted. (The Senate won.) The small differences between the two versions of the resolution were easily settled, and the conference report was adopted by votes of 65 to 29 in the Senate and 224 to 170 in the House. The final vote, in the House, came two days before the May 15 deadline for adopting the budget resolution.

MAKING THE RESOLUTION STICK

Once the budget targets for fiscal 1977 were in place, it was the Budget Committees' job to enforce them. Muskie remained much more aggressive than Adams. He concentrated almost all his attention on the tax bill, and his running battle with Long occupied the Senate for most of the summer. Adams, bolstered by his big win on the House floor, was more vigorous than he had been in 1975. But the tax bill moved through the House before the budget resolution was adopted, and Adams tried to enforce the resolution on a series of relatively minor issues, such as federal pensions and highway construction.

On the revenue side of the budget, the resolution was predicated on two key assumptions: a tax cut of $17.3 billion and $2 billion in new revenue through tax reform, for a net revenue decrease of $15.3 billion. The purpose of the tax cut was to lift the economy out of its continuing slump. The purpose of tax reform was quite different: to make the tax code more equitable. The Finance Committee prepared a tax bill that reached the budget resolution's target of a $15.3 billion cut in revenue—but not in the way that the report accompanying the budget resolution had suggested. It included only $1 billion in tax reform and a smaller tax cut than the Budget Committees had contemplated. Muskie and Bellmon, after getting the support of their Budget Committee, urged the Senate to modify the Finance Committee's bill to make it consistent with the resolution's assumptions. "This is not a contest between the Budget and Finance Committees," they maintained, but rather between two approaches to tax policy.[15] The Finance Committee felt otherwise. Sen. Lloyd Bentsen urged other committees to beat back the Budget Committee:

> If it [the Budget Committee] can deal with specificity and detail as to which taxes should be raised and which taxes should be lowered, then it has taken over the responsibilities of the Senate Finance Committee. . . . Let us not set a precedent here today or during these debates that creates a precedent of a substantial invasion of the jurisdiction of the Finance Committee. If that happens, you are going to see this same pattern followed in the Appropriations Committee and, finally, in the

other authorizing committees, and you will have seen the destruction, I think, of the budget reform act.[16]

Far from dictating every provision of the giant tax bill, Muskie replied, the budget resolution merely laid out two general directions for tax policy: tax cuts and tax reform. But Long reminded Muskie of his discussion with Sen. Bob Packwood, a Finance Committee member, when the first budget resolution was on the Senate floor. Packwood asked if the budget resolution would require the Finance Committee to report legislation with $2 billion worth of tax reform, and Muskie responded:

> The only mandatory number with respect to revenues is the revenue total that we have included. . . . We have, however, indicated in the report, as we are required, our view as to whether any revenue should be generated by tax reform. . . . We, of course, would like to have the Finance Committee look at the Budget Committee report to get whatever insight it chooses to take from the Budget Committee's recommendations and the basis for the Budget Committee's judgment. But in the last analysis, it is the Finance Committee's judgment. . . .[17]

When Muskie and Bellmon tried to increase the tax cut to make it conform with their interpretation of the budget resolution, they were defeated on a vote of 49 to 42. Long and Bentsen apparently had alarmed other committees about the threat of Budget Committee encroachment on their jurisdiction, for the chairman of the other major Senate committees voted 8 to 3 against the deeper tax cut. Budget Committee members, on the other hand, lined up 9 to 3 with their chairman. Sen. Warren G. Magnuson, the only committee chairman who also sat on the Budget Committee, supported Long.[18] However, a month later, when passions had subsided, Long did not try to block a similar amendment to deepen the tax cut.[19]

The real battles were fought over tax expenditures. Muskie unsuccessfully supported a series of amendments aimed at deleting old tax expenditures or new ones included in the Finance Committee's version of the tax bill. For example, a provision benefiting life insurance companies was upheld on a vote of 43 to 34, with Senate committee chairmen voting 8 to 3 in favor and Budget Committee members 7 to 4 against.[20] In fact, the tax bill was so loaded down on the Senate floor with new tax expenditures that instead of raising $1 billion through tax reform, it would have lost $300 million. One new tax expenditure that particularly upset Muskie was a tax credit for college tuition payments. The Budget Committee chairman, scarcely able to control his anger after the Senate approved that provision, said:

> It is quite clear to me that as far as the Internal Revenue Code is concerned, the Senate has indicated the budget process is meaningless. . . . May I say to my colleagues, you kicked the biggest hole in the budget process that you could conceivably kick. . . . I am going to sit down. I am tired of wasting my voice.[21]

But when the tax bill went to a conference committee of Senate Finance Committee and House Ways and Means Committee members, a remarkable thing happened. The bill, at least in its totals, came out looking just like the House version, which produced $1.6 billion through tax reform and cut taxes by the $17.3 billion recommended in the budget resolution. Feeling vindicated, Muskie said the final version of the tax bill "reflects the substantial impact of the new budget process."[22]

Was the budget process really decisive? Probably not, although it certainly focused attention as never before on the impact of tax expenditures on total federal revenue and the deficit. As Long himself admitted, "In several cases, we had to recede on Senate amendments in order to meet our revenue targets."[23] However, Long hardly gave up everything in conference. He defeated some of the House-passed tax reform measures to which he objected most strongly, and many of the tax reform provisions in the Senate version of the bill prevailed in conference. At the same time, Long had to abandon many of the new tax expenditures that the Senate had attached to the tax bill. But the Senate traditionally loads its tax bills with new tax expenditures—such as the college tuition credit—only to give them away in the end. That way a senator can vote for an item that is popular with his constituents without being responsible for making bad law. More than one senator has told Long during debate on a tax bill, "I'm going to vote for this one, Russell, because I know you'll get rid of it in conference." That's what happened in 1969 with the most recent big tax reform bill, and that's what happened in 1976.[24]

While Muskie and Long were locked in combat over the tax bill, Adams was fighting a series of skirmishes over particular spending items. In July, he asked ten committee and subcommittee chairmen to get busy on legislation to save money in the coming fiscal year. The savings would be necessary, Adams said, if Congress were to meet the spending targets of the first budget resolution. Mahon of Appropriations was not on the list, and some of the savings were items that the Appropriations Committee had sought for years. Most of the other savings had been proposed in March 15 reports by committees that wanted to demonstrate their desire to cut spending. As a rule, these committees could not agree on legislative specifics—for example, Medicaid reform got nowhere in the Interstate and Foreign Commerce Committee—and Adams did not press them. In fact, he worked hard for only two of the savings, and he obtained both, but only after ruffling the feathers of some other committees.

The first case was repeal of the 1-percent "kicker." Since 1969, retired federal workers had received an extra 1-percent increase in their pension benefits with every cost-of-living increase. Federal retirement benefits had gone up by 72 percent during a period when the cost of living had risen by only 56 percent. The Budget Committees assumed repeal of the 1-percent kicker in the first budget resolution for fiscal 1977.

But majorities of the House and Senate Post Office and Civil Service Committees, responsible for legislation affecting the benefits of retired federal workers, opposed repeal. To get around those committees, Sens. Lawton Chiles and Ernest F. Hollings, members of both the Appropriations and the Budget Committees, amended the appropriations bill for the legislative branch to include repeal of the 1-percent kicker. Muskie said the amendment was not a product of the Budget Committee, although he observed that it was consistent with the budget resolution.[25] In the House, repeal of the 1-percent kicker was a Budget Committee initiative. When the conference committee on the legislative appropriations bill retained repeal of the kicker, Adams supported it, and so did the House.[26]

Adams's second major target was a limit on spending for highway construction financed through the Highway Trust Fund, whose revenues came from highway user taxes. States whose highway construction projects won approval from the Transportation Department qualified for $9 in federal aid for every $1 of their own that they spent. When fiscal 1977 was about to begin, the trust fund had $11.9 billion available for highway construction, but the amount that actually would be spent would depend on how much the states qualified to receive. The House Appropriations and Budget Committees thought there should be greater control at the federal level over Highway Trust Fund outlays. Adams warned the House that a sudden jump in highway construction by the states would cause an increase in federal spending that would force up the deficit or crowd other programs out of the budget.[27] The Appropriations Committee included a $7.2 billion outlay ceiling for highway construction in its fiscal 1977 transportation appropriations bill.

On the House floor, Rep. James J. Howard, chairman of the Public Works and Transportation Subcommittee on Surface Transportation, offered an amendment to delete the ceiling, which he said would inhibit highway construction when unemployment in the construction industry was already high. The House accepted his amendment, 251 to 146.[28] The Senate included a $7.2 billion ceiling in its version of the transportation appropriations bill. When the bill went to a conference committee of House and Senate Appropriations Committee members, Adams urged conferees to support the ceiling. Howard was furious with Adams for betraying the House position, but the conference committee kept the ceiling. The House, by a vote of 226 to 167, agreed to abide by its decision.[29]

THE SECOND RESOLUTION

While Muskie and Adams were enforcing the first budget resolution, Congress was—for the most part—diligently meeting the deadlines laid out by budget reform. May 15 was the last day for committees to report legislation authorizing appropriations for fiscal 1977, and all authorizing committees in the House and most in the Senate met the deadline. Authorization bills were still subject to considerable change after May 15. But at least they were in a preliminary form that gave the House and Senate Appropriations Committees an idea of the kinds of programs for which they would be asked to appropriate funds. The Appropriations Committees were able to move ahead at their fastest pace in fifteen years. By the budget deadline of seven days after Labor Day—in this case, September 13—Congress had completed nine of its thirteen regular appropriations bills and advanced the other four nearly to completion. In addition, Congress was three days late with the mammoth tax bill that occupied the Senate for most of the summer, but by September 13 the House-Senate conference committee had finished its work and put the tax bill in its final form.

Timely action on the spending and tax bills enabled the Budget Committees—unlike the previous year—to prepare the second budget resolution on schedule. Legislation enacted during the summer had come close to the targets of the first resolution—in part because Congress had tried to hit them. "Congress is to be commended for its close adherence to the targets," the House Budget Committee said.[30]

Hitting the targets is not a sufficient reason for the second resolution to duplicate the first. As conceived by budget reform's authors, the second resolution should be a response to changing economic conditions, and the economy in September was far less healthy than Congress had predicted in its first resolution. The unemployment rate, instead of falling to 7 percent by the end of 1976, turned back up in June and reached a high of 7.9 percent in August. However, the Budget Committees were not alarmed enough to write new economic stimulus into the second resolution. They felt it would be prudent to wait for the recommendations of the Democratic president they expected to be elected in November. In addition, it was still the first year in which all the new budget procedures were in effect, and the Budget Committees' first goal was to complete all the steps. If they had sought more economic stimulus, they would have had to direct other committees to prepare new spending legislation or an additional tax cut. If the other committees had resisted, the budget process could have come unstuck.

So the Budget Committees wrote a second resolution whose spending ceilings and revenue floor were almost identical to the targets of the first. Both Budget Committees warned that a third resolution might be necessary early in 1977 if the economy continued to be sluggish. The House committee said, "The committee believes additional economic stimulus measures should be considered early next year if the slowdown in the recovery experience this spring continues during the third and fourth quarters of 1976."[31] The Senate passed its version of the second resolution by a vote of 55 to 23. Adams, continuing to draw new support for budget resolutions, got a vote of 227 to 151. A conference committee quickly reconciled the two versions, and the Senate adopted the conference report on September 15, the deadline set by the budget reform act. The House, busy with environmental legislation on September 15, adopted the resolution one day late.

THE THIRD RESOLUTION

Adoption of the second budget resolution was not the end of the congressional budget cycle for fiscal 1977. The economic slump continued, and Jimmy Carter, elected president in November, proposed a further tax cut and more spending for jobs programs even before his inauguration. When the 95th Congress convened in January 1977, it was clear that it would adopt a third budget resolution to make room for new economic stimulus.

But some housekeeping matters needed attention first. Adams, who intended to leave the House Budget Committee after his two-year term in any event, was appointed secretary of transportation in the new administration. Among the Democrats who had drawn four-year terms on the Budget Committee, Thomas L. Ashley of Ohio was the only serious contender for the chairmanship. But Robert N. Giaimo of Connecticut, one of the members with two-year terms, convinced the Democratic Caucus to extend his two years to four. In a contest between Ashley and Giaimo, the caucus elected Giaimo by a vote of 139 to 129. His election put the Budget Committee in the hands of an ethnic Democrat from the university town of New Haven. A solid liberal when he entered Congress in 1959, Giaimo swung toward the right when New Haven rebelled against urban renewal in the late 1960s, but by 1977 he was moving back again. As a member of the Appropriations Committee he had learned how the budget worked, and he also had acquired some of that committee's fiscal conservatism. He described himself in 1977 as a radical on civil liberties, but a fiscal moderate.

The Democratic side of the Budget Committee became more liberal and the Republican side more conservative as each party tried to counter the influence of the other. The new Democrats included some of the House's most thoughtful liberals—Joseph L. Fisher, Donald M. Fraser, Norman Y. Mineta, David R. Obey, Otis Pike, and Paul M. Simon. One of the new Republican committee members was John H. Rousselot, one of the half-dozen most conservative House members on fiscal matters, who had distinguished himself by trying to amend previous budget resolutions on the House floor to achieve what was then an impossibility—a balanced budget. At least one of the moderate Republicans who had supported budget resolutions from the beginning—Charles Whalen—did not even try to get on the Budget Committee because he knew that John Rhodes, the House Republican leader, wanted to load the committee with conservatives.

The Senate Budget Committee remained relatively stable. Muskie and Bellmon stayed on as chairman and Republican leader. Three committee members had failed to gain reelection, one resigned from the committee, and Walter F. Mondale had become vice president, but their replacements did not alter the character of the committee. However, the Democratic leadership had difficulty persuading Democrats to accept assignments on the Budget Committee, which offered none of the political advantages associated with committees with jurisdiction over programs popular with the voters.

The newly constituted Budget Committees wasted no time preparing a third budget resolution for fiscal 1977. It was only the second year of budget reform, and the Budget Committee chairmen felt somewhat embarrassed that a third resolution had already proved necessary. The eight Republicans on the House Budget Committee took the opportunity to accuse the committee of acting as a rubber stamp for spending proposals of every interest group, and especially of organized labor. "This resolution," the Republicans said, "tends to convert the budget process from an instrument of control over spending and revenue to an instrument of political expediency."[32]

But under the circumstances, it was difficult to imagine a Democratic Congress, with a Democrat in the White House for the first time in eight years, not moving to pump up the economy. If the budget process had not allowed for the possibility of a third resolution, Congress simply would have had to break the limits of the second, just as it broke its spending ceilings in the 1940s and made that budget reform experiment fail. The third resolution forced Congress to look seriously at the degree of economic stimulus it felt was appropriate. As Bellmon said:

> This third budget resolution demonstrates a strength, not a weakness, in the budget process. The process is flexible enough to permit adjustment when economic or emergency conditions warrant; however, the process is not so flexible as to allow for changes whenever an economic statistic moves in an adverse direction. It is anticipated that this resolution will prove to be a unique budgetary event, and that future years will require only the normal first and second budget resolutions.[33]

The House Budget Committee moved first to prepare a third budget resolution. Giaimo, leading his first markup, approached his job exactly as Adams had, presenting the committee with his own recommendation for the third resolution. "When we derived our figures," he explained, "we derived them from what we thought they would be, not from what we wanted to be in there."[34] Item by item, the committee discussed ten proposals for stimulating the economy, ranging in size from a $13.8 billion tax cut to $30 million for a program of part-time work for the elderly poor. No committee members objected as long as the committee simply made room for programs that had been recommended to it by other House committees. But no committee member was able to put anything into the resolution that might put a constraint on the legislation being prepared by another committee. Rousselot tried; he proposed a deeper, permanent tax cut as a way of reducing the size of government. The committee defeated Rousselot's effort after Pike, a Ways and Means Committee member, protested, "Now you're trying to write the package that Ways and Means is responsible for."[35]

The Senate Budget Committee also proceeded in its customary way. Without presenting any recommendations of his own, Muskie outlined to committee members the Carter proposals for economic stimulus and a smaller package that had been prepared by Senate Republicans. The two sets of recommendations gave committee members an excellent opportunity to debate fiscal policy—and they took advantage of it. They walked through the budget function by function, discussing the various proposals in considerable detail and generally settling upon functional spending totals designed to make room for the larger Carter package.

The two versions of the resolution had an easy time on the House and Senate floors. The vote in the Senate was 72 to 20, while Giaimo received a vote of 239 to 169 in the House. The two Budget Committees speedily reconciled the two versions in conference committee, and Congress completed work on the third budget resolution on March 3.

AND THE FOURTH

To the consternation of the Budget Committees, even the third resolution was not the end of the fiscal 1977 budget cycle. Scarcely a month after Congress adopted the third resolution, President Carter withdrew his support for the biggest component of his economic stimulus package—a $50 rebate for individual taxpayers—on grounds that the economy was improving on its own. Soon afterward, the Office of Management and Budget reported that fiscal 1977 outlays were falling short of its earlier estimate. Thus the third resolution's revenue total was $10 billion lower than necessary, and its outlay total was $9 billion too high. Neither circumstance required Congress to revise its third resolution, which simply set a minimum revenue level and a maximum for outlays. However, the new budget estimates meant that there was plenty of room for Congress to enact new and possibly irresponsible tax cuts and spending programs without violating its budget resolution. "As of this moment," Muskie said, "there is no discipline left in the 1977 budget resolution."[36] Bellmon, who had stressed when Congress adopted its third resolution that changes in budget policy should be infrequent, was particularly put out. "We tried to follow the President's lead," he complained, "and now we find ourselves in a bind."[37]

Both Budget Committees combined a revised third resolution for fiscal 1977—in effect, a fourth resolution—with the first resolution for fiscal 1978. But they took very different approaches. Persuaded by Muskie and Bellmon, the Senate left room for a tax cut in the event that the economic upturn of early 1977 proved ephemeral. But it revised outlays to reflect the administration's new estimates. The House, on the other hand, changed the fiscal 1977 revenue total in the belief that a tax rebate was unlikely without Carter's support, although Giaimo admitted that "it is unwise to make repeated changes in the policies we adopt in our budget resolutions."[38] At the same time, the House did not revise the outlay total; Giaimo wanted to wait for further estimates from the administration. In conference committee, Muskie agreed to give up the tax rebate when Giaimo said he would acknowledge the revised outlay total. The combination had the effect of reducing the fiscal 1977 deficit from $69.75 billion in the third resolution to $52.6 billion in the revision. The fourth resolution was adopted when the House gave final approval to the first resolution for fiscal 1978. The fiscal 1977 budget cycle came to an end on May 17—a year and four days after adoption of the first resolution for fiscal 1977.

CHAPTER 5

THE TWO BUDGET
COMMITTEES

THE HOUSE AND SENATE Budget Committees, the central instruments of budget reform, operated so differently in their
early years that it was as if they were working under two
budget reform acts. The House Budget Committee was exact-
ing; the Senate Budget Committee, free-wheeling. When the
House committee labored line by line through the budget, the
Senate committee criticized it for missing important issues of
fiscal policy and spending priorities. When the Senate committee focused on the big picture, the House committee said
it had lost sight of the pieces from which a budget is built.
Partisan divisions split the House's committee, while the
Senate's operated in a spirit of bipartisan togetherness. The
Senate Budget Committee was an aggressive, independent
force in the Senate; the House Budget Committee often acted
as an agent of others, sometimes the Appropriations Committee, sometimes the Democratic leadership.

In one sense, the two committees actually did operate under different laws. House Budget Committee members had to
rotate off the committee every four years, and some of them
represented important centers of House power—the Appropriations and Ways and Means Committees, the Democratic
and Republican leadership. The Senate Budget Committee,

on the other hand, was a committee like any other. Democrats on the House Budget Committee, reflecting the partisan division of the House, outnumbered Republicans by more than two to one. Senate Budget Committee Republicans were outnumbered by a smaller margin, and they formed a powerful alliance with southern Democrats. That alliance led to a bipartisanship that contributed to the independent role that the Senate Budget Committee was able to play. Finally, the distinctive personalities of the Budget Committee chairmen complemented the structural differences between the committees.

STRUCTURAL DIFFERENCES

Edmund Muskie, the first and only Senate Budget Committee chairman during the committee's early years, was an aggressive senator who had run for vice president in 1968 and nearly obtained the Democratic presidential nomination in 1972. In 1975, at the beginning of the 94th Congress, only twenty senators had more seniority than Muskie, who had served for sixteen years. Muskie had already been the chairman of subcommittees of all three of the committees on which he sat—Foreign Relations, Government Operations, and Public Works. He had been an author of air and water pollution legislation and revenue sharing—as well as the budget reform act itself.

Al Ullman, the House Budget Committee chairman for five months in 1974, had served in the House two years longer than Muskie had been in the Senate. But as the second-ranking Democrat on the Ways and Means Committee, Ullman operated in the shadow of Ways and Means chairman Wilbur Mills, who maneuvered Ullman into the chairmanship of the Budget Committee. Brock Adams, who succeeded Ullman in 1975, had been in the House for only ten years, and his only chairmanship was of a subcommittee of the lowly District of Columbia Committee. Robert Giaimo had eighteen years of service in the House when he followed Adams as Budget Committee chairman in 1977, but even that was not long enough to make him chairman of a subcommittee on the Appropriations Committee, on which he served. Neither Adams nor Giaimo was accustomed to dealing with the House elders who were the chairmen of the important House committees, and they treated them with deference.

If the personalities of the chairmen helped explain the aggressive posture of the Budget Committee in the Senate and the more passive nature of the one in the House, so did two vital differences in the makeup of the two committees. Most sections of the budget reform act were compromises between the House and the Senate, but each chamber was solely responsible for making the ground rules for its own Budget Committee. In the House, the makeup of the Budget Committee was dictated by a fear on the part of the Appropriations and Ways and Means Committees that the Budget Committee would take over the functions of the traditional spending and revenue committees. The Budget Committee was made the first in the House to have a rotating membership—no one could serve on it for more than four years in any ten. The Senate, rejecting a similar proposal, opted for permanent Budget Committee membership. "If rotating members of the committees had been desirable," said Sen. Sam Ervin, "it would have been done some time between the time the first Congress met in 1789 and the present date."[1]

The temporary nature of House Budget Committee membership detracted from the importance of assignment to that committee. The chairman could not use the Budget Committee to build a permanent power base in the House. He could not afford to antagonize too many colleagues who might be in a position to get even with him after he lost his chairmanship. Committee members—especially Republicans—were keenly aware of their temporary assignments. "Many committee members feel, 'This is a temporary assignment, so why should I give it my full time?'" said Delbert Latta, the committee's Republican leader.[2] Barber Conable, another committee Republican, said, "It is my impression . . . that most of the members of the Committee on the Budget, with the exception of the chairman and some of the very senior members, look at it as a secondary assignment and that it does not acquire the importance in the congressional lives of its members that was hoped when the Committee on the Budget was set up."[3]

In the Senate, Budget Committee membership was indefinite—and it was regarded as much more valuable. Muskie resigned from the prestigious Foreign Relations Committee to devote more time to the Budget Committee. In 1974, twenty-seven of the Senate's forty-two Republicans applied for the six Republican seats on the Budget Committee, and the Republican Conference, by assigning four of the seats to senators who were seeking reelection, showed that it felt Budget Committee membership was politically valuable. Henry Bellmon, who was just another conservative Republican from Oklahoma before budget reform, gained enormous influence and respect as the Republican leader of the Budget Committee.

A second structural difference between the two committees also served to weaken the committee in the House. The Senate Budget Committee, like all other Senate committees, was open to all senators whose party leadership would appoint them to a seat. But the House, as another precaution against an all-powerful Budget Committee, provided in the budget reform act that five Budget Committee members represent the Appropriations Committee, five be delegates from the Ways and Means Committee, and two serve as envoys from the House Democratic and Republican leadership. Only eleven committee members (increased to thirteen when committee membership was expanded to twenty-five in 1975) were to be chosen at-large from the entire House membership.

Thus twelve Budget Committee members in the House were representatives of other powerful legislative entities. As intended, these members tried to make sure the Budget Committee did not develop too much power of its own. Neal Smith of the Appropriations Committee fought a generally losing battle to keep the Budget Committee from recommending spending targets for individual appropriations accounts. Otis G. Pike of the Ways and Means Committee helped keep the Budget Committee from proposing specific tax policy in its third resolution for fiscal 1977. Tip O'Neill, as House Democratic leader, amended resolutions in 1975 and 1976 to make them appeal to liberal Democrats. Jim Wright, who followed O'Neill as Democratic leader in 1977, worked during preparation of the first resolution for fiscal 1978 for one of the leadership's key goals—restoration of funds for nineteen water resources projects that President Carter had requested be terminated.

The House Budget Committee acted as a servant of the Appropriations Committee when it worked for repeal of the 1-percent kicker and enactment of an outlay ceiling for highway construction in 1976. It was an instrument of the Democratic leadership early in 1977, when the Appropriations Committee was forced to beef up the jobs programs proposed by President Carter. It enhanced the considerable power that the Democratic leadership already enjoyed. In the Senate, by contrast, the Budget Committee antagonized the very committees that the House Budget Committee was structurally obligated to serve. In 1974, it fought with the Appropriations Committee for jurisdiction over presidential impoundment proposals. Two years later, it waged war with the Finance Committee over the tax bill. With no strong Democratic leadership to guide it, the Budget Committee struck out forcefully on its own.

Senate Budget Committee members also were members of other Senate committees, but they were not appointed by the other committees to represent them on the Budget Committee. Often they worked for higher spending totals for programs in their other committees' jurisdiction, but they did so on their own. On the other hand, the House Budget Committee members who represented the Appropriations and Ways and Means Committees and the Democratic and Republican leadership had to answer to the entities that appointed them. They kept the House Budget Committee from developing into the kind of independent force within the House that the Senate Budget Committee quickly became in the Senate.

PARTISANSHIP

The unique structure of the House Budget Committee also contributed to another striking difference between the two Budget Committees—the roles of their Republican members. The eight Republicans on the House Budget Committee, with no opportunity to make the Budget Committee their career, maintained an ideological opposition to big spending and big deficits. They were relatively senior and conservative, selected to offset the liberal slant that House Republican leader John Rhodes perceived on the Democratic side of the committee. The six Senate Budget Committee Republicans were relatively junior senators who felt they could use their committee membership to enhance their power in the Senate. They regularly voted with the committee rather than with their own ideological instincts, as when four of them supported the Budget Committee's challenge to the 1975 military procurement Bill. As John Ellwood and James Thurber wrote:

> Members of the Senate Budget Committee realize that their power in the Senate will be associated with the rise in stature and power of the Senate Budget Committee. Therefore, it is in the interest of Senate Budget Committee members to see to it that the budget resolutions reported out by the committee are successfully passed on the Senate floor. This motivation of self-interest goes a long way toward explaining the bipartisan nature of Senate Budget Committee proceedings.[4]

But other factors were at work as well, and not the least of them was simple arithmetic. Democrats outnumbered Republicans by ten to six on the Senate Budget Committee, but the six Republicans could be in the majority if they could get the support of the committee's three southern Democrats—Lawton Chiles, Ernest F. Hollings, and Sam Nunn in 1975–76. During markup of the first resolution for fiscal 1976, a coalition of Republicans and southern Democrats was on the winning side of a 9-to-6 vote that determined the defense target.[5] The same coalition set the targets for two important domestic functions—education, manpower, and social services and income security—and it controlled a 9-to-4 vote to cut Muskie's economic stimulus package from $8 billion to $4 billion.[6]

Before they took the resolution to the Senate floor, Muskie and Bellmon agreed to defend the committee's version in its entirety, although neither supported every provision. Thus Muskie voted against an amendment to increase the economic stimulus package, and Bellmon opposed efforts to reduce spending in domestic functions. From then on, Muskie and Bellmon worked as a team when budget resolutions went to the Senate floor. Republicans and southern Democrats continued to win a good share of the votes in committee, and Muskie did not waver from his determination to support on the floor those provisions that he opposed in committee. When the first resolution for fiscal 1978 went to the Senate floor, for example, he opposed amendments that he had supported in committee to increase spending for housing and community development. In return, Republican Budget Committee members J. Glenn Beall and Pete V. Domenici regularly joined Bellmon in support of budget resolutions. Only James L. Buckley and James A. McClure constantly opposed them, while Robert Dole voted for some and against others. On the floor, Republicans divided almost evenly; their biggest margin against a budget resolution in the first two years was 18 to 14 against the second resolution for fiscal 1977.

Bipartisanship never developed in the House. In 1975, Adams and the House Democratic leadership figured that there were two kinds of resolutions the House would approve: conservative ones supported by Republicans and conservative and moderate Democrats, and more liberal ones backed by moderate and liberal Democrats. They rejected the former option, which was similar to the course followed in the Senate, and attempted the latter.

They made it work because Democrats outnumbered Republicans seventeen to eight on the House Budget Committee. On rare occasions, the Republicans were able to get the support of four southern Democrats—Omar Burleson, Butler Derrick, Sam Gibbons, and Phil Landrum in 1975–76—plus Harold Runnels of New Mexico. That coalition asserted itself most significantly when, by a vote of 13 to 12, it set defense targets higher than the northern Democrats wanted for the first resolution for fiscal 1977. But on most domestic spending issues, the northern Democrats—in whose number was Tip O'Neill, the persuasive majority leader—were able to pick up the vote of at least one of the other Democrats. In these cases, the Democrats had no need to compromise to gain any Republican support, and the Republicans had nothing to gain by cooperating with the Democrats.

They cooperated only once, when Elford Cederberg and Barber Conable voted in committee to report the first resolution for fiscal 1976 to the House floor because Adams was unable to mobilize enough Democrats to keep the process moving in its first year. In every subsequent vote in committee or on the floor in 1975 and 1976, Budget Committee Republicans stood solidly against budget resolutions. Opposition from Republicans and southern Democrats—plus a handful of the most liberal Democrats—nearly doomed the first and second resolutions for fiscal 1976 on the House floor. Unlike Muskie, Adams did not have the luxury of enforcing budget resolutions that had won overwhelming approval.

As minority leader of the House Budget Committee, Latta led the Republican opposition. His position was simple: the House had failed to use budget reform to reduce spending and cut the deficit. He told the House in 1977:

While the Budget Committee may have succeeded in trimming the extravagances [such as the 1-percent kicker] out of the budget, it has all but failed to weed out the excesses. We have prevented the ship from sinking directly to the bottom of the sea, but it is still taking on water at an alarming rate.[7]

Latta was obeying the wishes of Republican leader Rhodes, who was responsible for placing Latta on the Budget Committee in the first place. Rhodes founded his opposition on the grounds that the Budget Committee had failed to "face up to their responsibility to hold the line on federal spending."[8] Rhodes in turn was seeking direction from the White House, as long as a Republican lived there. President Ford's position on the first resolution for fiscal 1977 was typical: he said he would have vetoed it as too costly if he had had the opportunity.[9] The unyielding position of the White House kept Budget Committee Republicans in line. Late in 1975, the Budget Committee staff tried to win over the three Republicans whom it regarded as the likeliest prospects: James Broyhill, Barber Conable, and James Hastings. The staff said Adams was having trouble getting 218 votes—a majority of the House—from Democrats alone, since some southern conservatives and a few northern liberals regularly opposed budget resolutions that appealed to the Democratic Party's moderates. But the three Republicans said they felt obliged to support President Ford.

Republicans on the Senate Budget Committee felt no such obligation. In fact, Henry Bellmon, the committee's Republican leader, grew quite hostile toward the White House. When the president vetoed a fiscal 1976 appropriations bill for the Labor and HEW Departments because it exceeded his budget request, Bellmon said:

I believe the president is wrong. Congress, as I am hopeful the president will one day fully understand, now has its own budgetary process. It is a good budgetary process. It is working. [This bill] is within the limits of this budgetary process, and it is sound reasoning for overriding the president's veto.[10]

By cooperating with the Democrats, the Republicans on the Senate Budget Committee were able to exert considerably more influence over the size and shape of budget resolutions than were their counterparts in the House. Conversely, House Democrats, having consciously decided to seek passage of budget resolutions without conservative support, were able to adopt more liberal resolutions than were Democrats in the Senate. Table 1 shows the relative impact of Republicans in the House and Senate on the fiscal policy of the first budget resolutions that were passed by the two chambers before a conference committee reconciled the separate versions.[11] House-passed versions of first budget resolutions —the budget process's key documents, which set overall spending and revenue targets for subsequent legislation— were consistently more economically expansive than Senate-passed versions. On the average of the first three years of budget reform, first budget resolutions as approved by the House included $1.4 billion more in budget authority and $3.8 billion more in outlays than those approved by the Senate. The deficits approved by the House were an average of $2.6 billion greater than those included in Senate resolutions.

Similarly, Republicans had more influence over spending priorities in the Senate, as can be seen from Table 2. New budget authority for defense was an average of $1.6 billion

Table 1 *First Budget Resolutions: Fiscal Policy*
(in billions of dollars)

	Fiscal 1976		Fiscal 1977		Fiscal 1978	
	House	*Senate*	*House*	*Senate*	*House*	*Senate*
Budget authority	$395.9	$388.6	$454.1	$454.9	$502.3	$504.6
Outlays	368.2	365.0	415.4	412.6	464.5	459.2
Revenue	298.2	297.8	363.0	362.4	398.1	395.7
Deficit	70.0	67.2	52.4	50.2	66.4	63.5

Note: The table compares the House-passed and Senate-passed versions of first budget resolutions during the first three years of the congressional budget process.
Source: House and Senate Budget Committees

Table 2   *First Budget Resolutions: Spending Priorities*
(in billions of dollars)

	Fiscal 1976		Fiscal 1977		Fiscal 1978	
	House	*Senate*	*House*	*Senate*	*House*	*Senate*
Defense spending:						
Budget authority	$100.5	$101.0	$112.0	$113.0	$117.1	$120.3
Outlays	90.2	91.2	100.6	100.9	109.9	111.6
Domestic spending:						
Budget authority	215.2	207.3	247.0	250.0	281.9	282.5
Outlays	203.4	199.7	224.4	225.3	251.5	247.1

Note: The table compares the House-passed and Senate-passed versions of first budget resolutions during the first three years of the congressional budget process. The domestic totals are the sums of the targets for five of the major domestic budget functions: commerce and transportation; community and regional development; education, training, employment, and social services; health; and income security.
Source: House and Senate Budget Committees

greater in first budget resolutions approved by the Senate than in those passed by the House, while defense outlays were $1 billion greater on the average. Republicans in both the Senate and the House worked for higher defense targets. By the same token, most Republicans in both chambers sought to reduce domestic spending, and they had more success in the Senate. Budget authority for five domestic budget functions was $1.4 billion a year lower in the Senate than the House, and outlays were $2.4 billion a year lower.

Second budget resolutions are not so useful for purposes of comparing Republican influence, because they largely reflected actions that Congress already had taken. But the third resolution for fiscal 1977, requested by newly inaugurated President Carter to make room for his proposals for economic stimulus, was a good barometer. The House approved $10.9 billion more in budget authority and $4.1 billion more in outlays than the Senate. The deficit in the House-passed resolution was $2.1 billion greater than in the version approved by the Senate. Once again, Democrats were relatively more influential in the House and Republicans relatively more effective in the Senate. (Appendix B shows a complete comparison of House-passed and Senate-passed budget resolutions, along with the final versions after conference committee action.)

In 1977, when Republicans lost control of the White House, Republican unity on the House Budget Committee gave way as some of the committee's newer Republicans recognized their previous lack of influence. Barber Conable, one of the Republicans who had participated in every budget resolution markup, spelled out the Republican philosophy that had prevailed to that point, arguing that it was the duty of the opposition party to put forward "its own agenda of reasonable, viable programs and the priorities it believes to be in the best interests of the country." But Conable accepted no responsibility to support the will of the majority when the Republican alternative was rejected. "You are the ones who control the legislative program for the next two years," he told the Democrats, "and you are the ones who should properly be held accountable to the people for the overall performance of the Congress."[12]

Two Republicans finally rejected this approach during the conference with the Senate on the first budget resolution for fiscal 1978. Defense was the key issue; the Senate version of the resolution provided $120.3 billion in budget authority, while the House version included only $117.1 billion. When House Democrats accepted a compromise of $118.5 billion— a higher figure than they originally felt the full House would approve—Republicans Marjorie S. Holt and Ralph S. Regula signed the conference report. It was the first time that House Republicans had supported a conference report on a budget resolution. Holt, who joined the Budget Committee in 1976, said she could not let a "small, ultraliberal minority" determine how much the nation should spend for defense. "We're kidding ourselves if we just sit back in our ivory tower and vote no," she said.[13] Regula, new to the committee in 1977, said Republicans were going to have to participate in the budget process if they expected to use it to balance the budget.[14] On the House floor, twenty-eight Republicans—a record—voted for the conference report. About an equal number of the more liberal Democrats deserted. Thus the House majority that supported the resolution had shifted to the right.

However, Republicans had reverted to form by the time of the second resolution for fiscal 1978. The second resolution contained little that was different from the first, except for several billion dollars in new revenue from increased energy and social security taxes. That was enough to turn all but four House Republicans against the second resolution.

Bipartisan support for budget resolutions in the Senate helped explain why the Senate Budget Committee was able to enforce resolutions more aggressively and openly than the House committee. Muskie knew that when he went to the Senate floor to challenge another committee, Bellmon would be right beside him. Adams, on the other hand, feared any action that would cost him votes on the next budget resolution. Their different points of view were reflected in the ways they compared action on spending legislation with the spending total in the most recent budget resolution. In frequent reports to the House, the House Budget Committee compared the resolution with spending bills already enacted or reported by committees. The difference told House committees how much room remained as they prepared further legislation. The Senate Budget Committee, in weekly reports prepared for it by the Congressional Budget Office, showed the Senate what would happen if all potential spending—legislation under consideration by other committees—were added to spending already enacted or reported by a Senate committee. The combination of potential and actual spending often exceeded the most recent budget resolution, and the effect was to encourage restraint.

When they had a serious disagreement with the legislation of another committee, Muskie and the Senate Budget Committee did not hesitate to go public. The two most important early cases concerned the 1975 military procurement bill and the 1976 tax bill. The strategy of seeking the spotlight was the result of a conscious decision in 1975, when Muskie hoped that his simultaneous opposition to the military procurement and school lunch bills would show he was willing to trim social programs as well as defense spending when the integrity of the budget resolution was at stake. "Our victories on the military procurement bill and the child nutrition bill convinced people that we meant business," said John T. McEvoy, then the committee's general counsel.[15]

The House Budget Committee, meanwhile, tried to work with other House committees in private to help them keep their spending legislation consistent with the most recent resolution. Only once in his two years as chairman did Adams go to the House floor to oppose another committee's legislation —the 1975 Postal Service reorganization bill. As time passed, the Senate Budget Committee grew more adept at operating at the committee-to-committee level to head off disputes before they turned into confrontations on the Senate floor. Budget Committee staff members became more familiar with the operating procedures of other committees, and other committees grew more comfortable with the Budget Committee.

The Senate Budget Committee enforced budget resolutions not only on spending bills—that is, appropriations bills and backdoor spending legislation—but also on authorization bills, which merely set spending ceilings for subsequent appropriations bills. The military procurement bill, the subject of the Senate Budget Committee's first big enforcement battle in 1975, was an authorization bill. Muskie maintained that it was important to hold the line on that authorization bill because Congress traditionally appropriated nearly all the funds that were authorized for the military. On other occasions, the Budget Committee refrained from enforcing budget resolutions on authorization bills, especially when it felt Congress would not appropriate all the funds that would be authorized. Such was the case with a 1975 authorization bill for the Land and Water Conservation Fund and a 1977 bill authorizing funds for the Energy Research and Development Administration.[16]

The House Budget Committee never tried to stop authorization bills; in fact, Adams was reluctant even to comment on their relationship to the latest budget resolution. When he was asked to talk about the original House Armed Services Committee version of the 1975 military procurement bill, Adams merely found it "interesting" that it was "some $1.3 billion above the comparable target related to the budget resolution."[17] Asked to compare the conference committee version of the bill with the resolution, he said, "I have rarely commented on authorization bills, because, as I stated during House debate on this measure, the function of such bills is to set upper limits on budget authority."[18]

WRITING THE RESOLUTIONS

When the two Budget Committees prepared the resolutions that they would later be called upon to enforce, they could hardly have taken more different approaches. In the House, where most members are legislative specialists, the Budget Committee built the congressional budget from the ground up. It computed spending for the nearly eleven hundred accounts of the budget, which ranged in size in fiscal 1977 from $75 billion for social security to $10,000 for the Treasury Department's check forgery insurance fund. Senators, forced by the smaller size of the Senate to be generalists, steered their Budget Committee away from such detail. The Senate Budget Committee tried to set spending totals without determining the size of the components.

In the Senate Budget Committee, the starting point for the first budget resolution was current policy, which the Budget Committee defined as the spending and revenue levels that would result in the next fiscal year from a continuation of current programs plus inflation.[19] The committee staff presented its members with the computation by the Congressional Budget Office of the cost of maintaining current policy in each of the sixteen budget functions. In addition, it identified major proposals for change in the president's budget request and the March 15 reports of other Senate committees. Budget Committee members took it from there. Typically, one member proposed budget authority and outlay totals above or below current policy, with few specifics as to the programs that should be cut or augmented. Other members might propose different totals. Often the member who took the lead on a particular function was one who served on another committee that dealt with programs in that function. For example, Alan Cranston, a member of the Veterans' Affairs Committee, always dominated debate on the veterans function. Sometimes the leader was a Budget Committee member who was listening to the lobbyists who tried to influence the shape of the congressional budget. When Ernest Hollings proposed increases in President Carter's request for fiscal 1978 defense spending, he had been contacted by defense lobbyists who included Secretary of Defense Harold Brown. On the revenue side of the budget, committee members looked at the grand total and judged whether economic conditions dictated an increase or a decrease in tax rates. They also decided whether total tax expenditures should be cut through tax reform.

The House Budget Committee's staff prepared for each budget resolution by estimating spending in the coming fiscal year for the nearly eleven hundred budget accounts. For many accounts, the staff got different estimates from different sources—the president's budget, the March 15 reports from other House committees, the Congressional Budget Office, and its own analyses. When the cause was a policy dispute in a major account, the committee chairman made the choices, much as the director of the Office of Management and Budget sets tentative budget totals for the executive departments and agencies before the president makes the final decisions. The result was the chairman's recommendation for the budget resolution. Most Budget Committee members saw the chairman's recommendation for the first time on the day when the committee began meeting to mark up a resolution to send to the House floor. The chairman showed his committee the precise components of his recommendation, which encouraged debate of individual items in the budget. During markup of the first resolution for fiscal 1978, committee members proposed outlay changes as small as $17 million for community services jobs for older Americans and $2 million for raises for highly paid federal employees.

The House Budget Committee was convinced that its approach was the only way to prepare a congressional budget. Adams said there was no way to decide how much money the government should spend in total without asking how much it should spend for the programs that make up that total.[20] The committee staff found the resolutions prepared by the Senate Budget Committee to be so vague as to be meaningless. Staff members were unable to compare their versions of budget resolutions with those of the Senate for purposes of reaching compromises in conference committee. When they asked whether the Senate's first resolution for fiscal 1976 included a 5-percent raise or an 8.66-percent raise for military employees, they found that the Senate Budget Committee could not tell them. They wondered how the Senate Budget Committee could enforce a budget resolution when it could not measure the resolution's components. They believed the Senate committee used inaccurate numbers when it challenged spending bills—for example, the 1975 military procurement bill—for exceeding the most recent budget resolution.

However, the House Budget Committee had to pay a high price for its line-by-line approach to the budget. Not only did it regularly get bogged down in debate of minor budgetary issues, but it also aroused the concern of Appropriations Committee chairman George Mahon, who did not appreciate the Budget Committee's tendency to tread on his committee's jurisdiction. Ironically, the House Budget Committee, which in most respects was careful not to antagonize other House committees, adopted an approach to the budget that hardly could have been calculated to be more troublesome to the Appropriations Committee. Some other House committees, eager to make their legislation consistent with the congressional budget, welcomed the detail and asked for more. John M. Murphy, chairman of the Merchant Marine and Fisheries Committee, asked Giaimo for the effect of the fiscal 1978 budget resolution on specific budget items under his committee's jurisdiction.[21] At the same time, some Budget Committee members complained that their committee was using the old, piecemeal technique for arriving at budget totals. "We established the Committee on the Budget," said Regula, "to avoid that very process."[22]

The Senate Budget Committee was equally convinced that only its approach guaranteed that the budget process would focus congressional attention on broad issues of fiscal policy and spending priorities. "It is easy to slip into discussion of individual programs or line items in the budget," Muskie said. "It is tempting to forget about the broad priority questions and to try to guarantee that our favorites are in the budget. . . . As this debate goes forward, let us not try to create a legislative history which guarantees the funding of this program but not that program. That work will be done in our other committees and on the floor."[23] When necessary, Muskie's staff was able to interpret the implications of a budget resolution for a particular spending bill. That enabled Muskie to be aggressive in demanding that individual bills conform to the resolution. At the same time, it prevented the Senate Budget Committee from getting so mired in detail that it lost sight of the big picture.

COMMITTEE STAFFS

In considerable measure, the diametrically opposed styles of the two Budget Committees were products of their staffs. The House Budget Committee felt it needed a staff of considerable technical expertise to compensate for the rapid turn-over of committee members, who would not have time to become expert in the complexities of the federal budget. The Senate Budget Committee, by contrast, was more willing to rely on the Congressional Budget Office for whatever technical assistance it needed. It chose a staff whose long suit was its political savvy.

For the House Budget Committee's first staff director, Ullman chose Walter Kravitz, an expert on the legislative branch who had worked for seventeen years with the nonpartisan Congressional Research Service, an arm of the Library of Congress. Ullman knew of Kravitz by reputation only; he chose him for his long-demonstrated appreciation of the need to strengthen budget-making in Congress.[24] Kravitz happened to be a Democrat, but he pursued his new duties in the same nonpartisan spirit that prevailed at the Congressional Research Service. "As I understand it, the chairman doesn't want the Budget Committee to produce a Democratic budget or a Republican budget," Kravitz said soon after joining the Budget Committee. "He wants it to produce a congressional budget, and that's the kind of approach I'm most comfortable with."[25]

Under the direction of Ullman and John Rhodes, the Republican leader not only of the House but also of the Budget Committee in 1974, the committee established an almost entirely nonpartisan staff experienced in the enormous complexities of the federal budget. Except for four staff members assigned exclusively to the Democratic committee members and two for the Republicans, the entire staff of about sixty persons was to serve both the Democrats and the Republicans. The key operating units were those that generated information about the spending side of the budget (headed by Bruce Meredith, formerly of the House Appropriations Committee staff) and that analyzed tax policy and the budget's relationship to the economy (under the direction of Nancy H. Teeters, formerly of the Brookings Institution). Among the few committee members who wanted a more partisan staff was Brock Adams, who feared Ullman's approach would produce "bland consensus."[26] When Adams succeeded Ullman as chairman in early 1975, he kept the staff structure intact, with Kravitz at its head. However, Adams and Kravitz were not a good match; the chairman perceived the staff director as Ullman's man, and Kravitz was uncomfortable with Adams's decision to seek a congressional budget that would appeal to the moderate and liberal Democratic majority—if not to the conservatives—in the House. Kravitz returned to the Congressional Research Service after a year with the Budget Committee, and George Gross, who as general counsel had been second in command on the committee staff, succeeded him. As counsel to the House Banking and Currency Subcommittee on Housing for five years before joining the Budget Committee, Gross was more at home with Capitol Hill politics than Kravitz had been.

In 1977, both Democrats and Republicans felt they were not getting enough political advice from the Budget Committee staff. Republicans found their own two-man staff ineffective, and they felt the nonpartisan staff was more willing to help the Democrats than themselves. During preparation of the first resolution for fiscal 1977, Latta sarcastically referred to Nancy Teeters as "our liberal economist."[27] The four Democratic staff members proved to be awkward appendages to the committee staff when their Democratic sponsors rotated off the committee. When Giaimo became committee chairman in 1977, he kept Gross at the head of the nonpartisan staff. But he also increased the partisan component of the staff by allowing a personal staff member for each of the committee's seventeen Democrats and eight Republicans.

The top Senate staff never shared the nonpartisan credo of Kravitz and the House staff. For staff director, Muskie chose Douglas J. Bennet, Jr., an unsuccessful Democratic candidate for Congress in 1974 and former administrative assistant to Democratic Senators Thomas F. Eagleton and Abraham Ribicoff. When Bennet left in 1977 to become an assistant secretary of state, he was succeeded by John McEvoy, who had been the committee's general counsel. McEvoy, a political strategist, had been Muskie's administrative assistant in 1971 and had served with his unsuccessful presidential campaign in 1972. Bennet and McEvoy set up a committee staff similar in structure to that of the House, with Sidney Brown in charge of the spending unit and Arnold H. Packer as chief economist. As individuals, the Senate staff members generally were less familiar with the technicalities of the budget than were their House counterparts, although many of them were better versed in broad program objectives and accomplishments. In addition to the central staff, each committee member appointed a staff aide of his own, for a total staff of about seventy-five. Bellmon appointed Robert Boyd as Republican staff director. Working side by side in the preparation of material for the committee, Bennet and Boyd brought to the staff the same bipartisanship that developed among the members of the Senate Budget Committee.

CHAPTER 6

THE CONGRESSIONAL
BUDGET OFFICE

"INFORMATION," SAID SEN. Lee Metcalf during debate of the budget reform act, "is the name of the game in budget control."[1] Before 1974, the president controlled the information. With no source of its own, Congress had to go to the executive branch when it wanted to know how much a program would cost. If the president opposed the program, he could make it appear unattractive by estimating its cost at an artificially high level. Congress had no way to challenge him.

When it enacted budget reform, Congress sought to create its own sources of budgetary information. In particular, it established the Congressional Budget Office to provide for Congress the same kinds of budget estimates that the Office of Management and Budget supplied to the president. The roughly two hundred staff members of the CBO, along with the staffs of the new Budget Committees, broke the executive branch's monopoly on budgetary information. Under Alice M. Rivlin, its first director, the CBO quickly established itself as highly expert in the complexities of the federal budget. Not only did the Congressional Budget Office perform much of the mathematics that was vital to the new congressional budget process, but it also developed into one of the most capable shops in town for analyzing the pros and cons of alternative federal policies. The first two comprehensive studies of the CBO's performance, both completed before the new office was even two years old, found that it was already providing Congress with high-grade budget and policy analysis.[2]

Indeed, the very quality of the CBO's work—and its director's flair for calling public attention to it—attracted a great deal of congressional criticism. Republicans did not like to be told that one of the favorite themes of the Ford administration —that the spending policies of the Democratic Congress were leading to bankruptcy—was ill founded. Democrats did not like to hear that the energy program advanced by the Carter administration was too weak to meet the administration's own goals. But Congress heard all this and more from the CBO.

As the director of a new arm of Congress—and a photogenic director at that—Rivlin found herself besieged by the media. She refused requests to discuss her own views of either the budget or the role of women on Capitol Hill. But she did not hesitate to try to educate the public about the new budget process and the work that her office was doing, even when that work was at odds with Democratic or Republican ideology. Unfortunately for Rivlin, Congress is populated by 535 men and women who would rather see themselves than their employees on television and in the newspapers. The jealousy with which Congress reacted to Rivlin's publicity posed the single greatest threat to the CBO in its infant years, overshadowing most considerations of the quality of the CBO's work. Opposition to the new office reached a crescendo late in 1975, when the House Appropriations Committee heard a proposal to wipe out nearly half of the organization that Rivlin had established. But the CBO weathered the storm with only slight damage, and it was left free to go about the business of helping Congress make its budget process succeed.

After the 1975 crisis the quality of the CBO's work improved steadily. But like the congressional budget process itself, the greater importance of the CBO was in its potential.

If the CBO supplied Congress for the first time with its own source of budgetary information, Congress did not always use it as much as it might have. On the one hand, the CBO's computations of budget estimates, vital to the day-to-day operation of the budget process, won wide acceptance on Capitol Hill. But Congress did not find the CBO so helpful in its other major role—analyzing alternative courses of federal policy. The fault lay partly with the CBO, which did not know what kinds of information Congress would find useful and sometimes contributed its best studies too late to affect decisions. But Congress, many of whose members and staffs were not interested in policy analysis, had to share the blame. Rivlin, a policy analyst herself, had been determined from the beginning to make her specialty one of the CBO's central functions. Halfway into her four-year term at the CBO, it was not entirely clear that she had succeeded.

ONE OF A KIND

The Congressional Budget Office was a unique institution, substantially different from both the executive branch's budget office and the other staff support agencies of Congress. The Office of Management and Budget, the central budget shop for the executive branch, served one master—the president. Especially when that president was Richard Nixon, the OMB was at the vortex of executive branch decision-making. It was an active participant when the administration was developing policy, more often than not recommending thrift when executive departments and agencies sought authority for more spending. Even on issues for which budget was not a central concern, the OMB tried to mold policy into a consistent package of presidential programs. After presidential policy was made, the OMB became its public advocate, particularly when policy required congressional approval. The OMB director appeared frequently in congressional hearing rooms.

The CBO, on the other hand, served not one master but 535—100 senators and 435 representatives. It could recommend no particular policy lest it alienate that policy's opponents. Its influence on Capitol Hill depended on its credibility, which would dissolve if Congress perceived it as just another liberal or conservative mouthpiece. The budget reform act required only that the CBO's staff be nonpartisan —not chosen because of party affiliation. But from the first, Rivlin intended to make the CBO impartial as well. A liberal herself, she vowed not to utter a liberal word as CBO director. "That's one of the costs of taking this job," she said.[3]

Unlike the OMB, the CBO was not a center of decision-making. Congress was not about to let an office of unelected staff members take over the job of deciding federal budget policy. The CBO's role was merely to compute the costs of possible courses of policy, and the advantages and disadvantages of each. The new office could not choose which course to follow; indeed, it could not even recommend which course Congress should choose. As C. William Fischer, one of Rivlin's first assistants, wrote, "CBO is to be neutral on outcomes, even with regard to the cost, but to clearly identify and illuminate what the implications of alternative actions are, including the costs."[4]

If the CBO did not behave like the OMB, neither did it function in the pattern of the other three staff offices of Congress. The CBO played a central role in a vital congressional decision-making process. It could do no more than provide Congress with information—as was the case with the other three staff offices. The General Accounting Office, established by the 1921 Budget and Accounting Act to make sure the executive branch spent funds as Congress had decreed, developed a capacity to perform policy analysis. The Congressional Research Service, which was an arm of the Library of Congress, and the Office of Technology Assessment, which had a board of directors composed of fourteen members of Congress, had a similar capacity, the former in the full range of federal policy, the latter in a limited field. But the GAO, CRS, and OTA were not essential actors in any part of the legislative process. Congress could operate, although not in so well-informed a manner, without them. But it could not maintain its budget process without the information provided by the CBO.

GETTING STARTED

The Congressional Budget Office was a creation of the Senate. When the House passed its version of budget reform legislation in 1973, it provided for the establishment of a Legislative Budget Office that would serve as a joint staff for the new Budget Committees, which would have no other staffs of their own. The nonpartisan Legislative Budget Office would function much as the staff of the Joint Committee on Internal Revenue Taxation operated as a body of experts on tax matters for the House Ways and Means and Senate Finance Committees. Its duties would be limited to providing technical expertise related to the budget. But in the Senate, budget reform legislation allowed the Budget Committees to have staffs of their own. The Congressional Office of the Budget, as established by the Senate's legislation, would perform tasks beyond those that could be undertaken by the Budget Committees' own staffs. In particular, it would analyze broad policy issues—particularly but not exclusively economic issues—with budgetary implications. The conference committee that wrote the final version of the budget reform bill settled on a hybrid name—the Congressional Budget Office. But in all other respects, the new office was just what the Senate ordered.

And Alice Rivlin was the director whom the Senate chose to lead the CBO in the direction the Senate desired. The House Budget Committee's first choice for CBO director was Phillip S. Hughes, an assistant comptroller general of the General Accounting Office and former deputy director of the

Bureau of the Budget. An expert technician, Hughes reflected the House Budget Committee's wish that the CBO concentrate on helping Congress wade through the complexities of the federal budget. Where Hughes had served both Democrats and Republicans in the Bureau of the Budget, Rivlin was clearly identified as a liberal Democrat. An economist by training, she had served as assistant secretary of HEW for planning and evaluation during the final year of the Johnson administration. With the Brookings Institution, she was an author of three volumes laying alternatives to the Nixon budgets of 1972, 1973, and 1974.[5] Sen. Edmund Muskie, chairman of the Senate Budget Committee, felt that Rivlin, more than Hughes, could help Congress turn the budget requests of President Ford into Democratic budgets. The House and Senate Budget Committees remained deadlocked through 1974. But early in 1975, Brock Adams acceded to Muskie's choice shortly after becoming House Budget Committee chairman.

In establishing her Congressional Budget Office, Rivlin was handicapped by her late start. The Budget Committees, organized six months before her appointment, had their staffs largely in place before Rivlin was able to begin selecting hers. "Each Budget Committee was staffed to provide much of the technical expertise that the [budget reform] act apparently intended CBO to provide for both," the House Commission on Information and Facilities found. "Especially on the House side, Budget Committee staffing was viewed as basically self-sufficient except for such work as the volume production of scorekeeping and bill-costing data. To some extent, therefore, it appears that CBO staff initially was sometimes viewed as rivals rather than collaborators."[6] The Budget Committee staffs were not only competent but large— about seventy-five strong in the Senate and sixty in the House at the outset. Their existence merely confirmed Rivlin's determination to provide not only the relatively routine budget estimates that the Budget Committees would need but also the kind of policy analysis that she felt would enrich the budget process.

Rivlin acquired a staff that was long on budget and program expertise but short on experience in working with Congress. She tried to find staffers familiar with the peculiar customs of Capitol Hill, but she found it difficult for the CBO, as a sort of congressional think tank, to attract persons who enjoyed wheeling and dealing in the halls of Congress. Rivlin herself had no experience on Capitol Hill, and neither did any of her top staff members except one: Stanley L. Greigg, head of the office of intergovernmental relations, had been a Democratic congressman from 1965–67. As her deputy Rivlin chose an economist with a background quite similar to her own. Robert A. Levine had been president of the New York City Rand Institute, and he had served in the Johnson administration as an assistant director of the Office of Economic Opportunity.

Levine notwithstanding, Rivlin sought staff members with diverse backgrounds and views. But she found it particularly difficult to please congressional conservatives who wanted her to locate economists outside the traditional Keynesian mold. Few such economists existed, and those who did were more likely to choose the private sector than the federal government as their employer. In the first year of the new budget process, James Buckley and James McClure, the two most conservative Republicans on the Senate Budget Committee, wrote, "Recent [CBO] studies appear to utilize [economic] models which are representative of a single economic school of thought, to the exclusion of other widely held viewpoints and models which reflect them. . . . It is our opinion that the initial efforts to secure . . . diversity within the CBO have not been pursued with sufficient vigor."[7]

But on the whole, the CBO staff that Rivlin recruited received high marks from other congressional staff members and outsiders. For example, William M. Capron of Harvard University found the CBO staff "extremely able."[8]

AMBUSH IN THE HOUSE

Not surprisingly, the CBO encountered its most formidable opposition in the House, not in the Senate. Despite Rivlin's pledge of impartiality the CBO quickly picked up a reputation for straying beyond neutral budget and policy analysis and into the forbidden territory of policy advocacy. On close inspection, the charge was without substantial merit. But even the appearance of bias led to a serious crisis for the CBO in the House.

One early source of the CBO's image as an advocate of liberal policy was its first economic report, presented to Congress on June 30, 1975.[9] Before submitting the report in final form, Rivlin circulated a draft to the Budget Committees for their comments. Some committee members, especially House Republicans, felt the draft overemphasized the need for economic stimulus to combat recession, at the expense of an analysis of the desirability of economic restraint to control inflation. The CBO revised the report accordingly, but the press still mistakenly concluded that the final version recommended a particular economic policy. The *Washington Star's* headline read, "$15 billion tax cut urged to offset oil price rise."[10] In fact, the report urged nothing at all, but headlines of this sort were enough to anger congressional conservatives.

Later that year, a neutral CBO estimate of defense spending was misinterpreted to appear biased against military growth. Sen. Alan Cranston had asked the CBO to compare the House version of the fiscal 1976 defense appropriations bill with the defense target of the first budget resolution. Using the set of assumptions about defense programs that Cranston had requested, the CBO computed that the House-passed bill was $932 million over the budget resolution. Cranston issued a press release announcing that Rivlin found the defense bill to be in excess of the resolution. The implication: Rivlin felt the defense bill should be cut. That implication found its way into a number of newspaper stories, and other senators and representatives were dismayed to read that the CBO was recommending that they cut defense spending. Actually, the CBO had done no such thing. "CBO itself took no position on the House-passed bill," Cranston conceded, "and made no recommendation with respect to that bill."[11] But his explanation came too late to erase the impression that the CBO had tried to squeeze down the defense budget.

Rivlin's ability to attract publicity aroused the jealousy of many members of Congress, who quickly found themselves less well known to the public than the unelected director of the Congressional Budget Office. In her first months on the job, Rivlin had a knack for making controversial statements in public. She charged in a 1975 speech that President Ford had provoked a "procedural confrontation" with Congress by insisting that Congress promptly adopt a spending ceiling for fiscal 1977, even though the budget process did not require Congress even to adopt a target for another seven months. She also took issue with some of the budget estimates upon which Ford's recommendation was based.[12] Republican members of Congress did not appreciate criticism of their president by their own budget director.

Unhappiness with the CBO converged on Rivlin's request in a fiscal 1976 appropriations bill for authority to hire a staff of 259 persons (compared with about six hundred in the OMB), more than even she had contemplated when she assumed her job. The budget reform act was silent about the number of persons who should work for the CBO. The Senate staff members who wrote the CBO into the act foresaw a staff of no more than a hundred, a figure that seemed reasonable to Muskie at the time.[13] Just before her appointment as director, Rivlin said the Budget Committees had given her a figure of 150 as a guideline, but she said she did not intend to hire that many persons immediately, lest her decisions be too hasty.[14] However, Rivlin quickly realized that the demands placed upon the CBO by the budget reform act would require a staff of 150 and then some. By October 1975, she had acquired a staff of 175 and committed jobs to another eighteen persons. She asked Congress for authority to expand the CBO staff to a total of 259. "We cannot do the job required of us," she told the House Appropriations Committee, "with the number of people we now have."[15]

Many members of the House Appropriations Subcommittee on the Legislative Branch disagreed. Its chairman, Rep. Bob Casey, complained that the CBO was doing more than responding to congressional requests for information.[16] Rivlin pointed out that the budget reform act allowed the CBO to initiate policy studies, and she added, "I don't think we want to be looking at kooky things or things nobody is considering."[17] Rep. Lawrence Coughlin charged that other congressional support offices could perform much of the CBO's work. Rivlin replied that the budget reform act assigned many tasks specifically to the CBO.[18] Rep. Elford Cederberg contended that a recent CBO economic report recommended that Congress increase federal spending. "No sir, it does not," Rivlin replied, adding that the report analyzed the consequences of a tax increase as well as a spending increase.[19] Rep. Robert Giaimo, a member of the Appropriations Subcommittee as well as the Budget Committee, was Rivlin's principal supporter. Adams, wary of taking a position that might alienate other House members in large numbers, merely submitted a statement in support of Rivlin's budget request for the Appropriations Committee's hearing record.

Congressman Coughlin, a Republican, proposed to cut the CBO staff to 123 by keeping the staff members who performed budget estimates but eliminating the three CBO divisions for policy analysis. The subcommittee rejected the Coughlin proposal, which would have left Rivlin without the divisions that she regarded as especially important. Instead, the subcommittee decided to freeze the CBO staff at 193. Its

decision was confirmed by the full Appropriations Committee, the House, and ultimately the Senate as well.

After the 1975 crisis, the CBO's relations improved with
Congress in general and the House Appropriations Subcommittee on the Legislative Branch in particular. Rep. George
E. Shipley, a CBO supporter, replaced Casey as the subcommittee's chairman in 1976. When Rivlin appeared before the
subcommittee that year, it did not repeat the battering that it
had administered in 1975. Coughlin, Rivlin's toughest critic
the previous year, was impressed with the CBO's efforts to
avoid duplication with other congressional support offices—
his biggest concern in 1975. He even commended Rivlin for
maintaining objectivity on policy issues.[20] The subcommittee
—and Congress as a whole—allowed the CBO staff to grow
to 208 in fiscal 1977, a figure that Rivlin said she could live
with indefinitely.

But Rivlin's flair for publicity continued to upset a significant number of members of Congress. Muskie, unconcerned
over the attention Rivlin received from the media, said at-
tracting notice to the CBO's work was an important part of
her job.[21] In the House, however, it was another story. Rep.
Jack Brooks, chairman of the House Commission on Information and Facilities, personally wrote the summary of the commission's report on the CBO, which declared in its first
paragraph, "The Congressional Budget Office maintains too
high a profile. Its willing visibility, unique among the legislative branch support agencies, threatens seriously to impair
the usefulness and integrity of a highly promising and pro-
ductive policy research agency."[22] Giaimo, who became
House Budget Committee chairman in 1977, did not personally object to Rivlin's publicity, but other House members
pressured him to try to silence the CBO director. When she
appeared before a Budget Committee oversight hearing,
Giaimo complained about a press conference that she had just
held to announce the startling conclusion of the latest piece

of policy analysis: that President Carter's energy program was not tough enough to meet the energy conservation goals that the president himself had set. Rivlin explained that House and Senate committees had requested the CBO study and approved the holding of the press conference. Press conferences, she said, were a useful way for the CBO to disseminate information. "I have been very careful never to make a recommendation of what the Congress ought to do," she added. "That isn't easy, because members of Congress kept asking me to do it."[23] Giaimo was satisfied for the moment, but the concern over the CBO's penchant for publicity seemed likely to continue for at least as long as Rivlin remained its director.

BUDGET ANALYSIS

The controversy over Rivlin's appearances on television and in the newspapers diverted attention from the CBO's fundamental tasks. The budget reform act directed the CBO to provide Congress with two basic kinds of information—budget analysis and policy analysis. More specifically, these were the CBO's main duties:

• Budget analysis:

—to keep Congress regularly informed of how the legislation it has enacted compares with the most recent budget resolution; this is called the scorekeeping function (Sections 202 [e] and 308 [b] of the budget reform act);

—to help committees that report spending and tax expenditure legislation—especially the Appropriations, Ways and Means, and Finance Committees—to compare their legislation to the most recent resolution (Section 308 [a]);

—to project for five years the costs of carrying out the provisions of every authorizing bill reported by a House or Senate committee (Section 403);

—to issue an annual report soon after the beginning of each fiscal year, projecting total spending, revenue and tax expenditures for the next five years (Section 308 [c]).

• Policy analysis:

—to report annually by April 1 on alternative budget courses that Congress might pursue in the coming fiscal year, with an emphasis on fiscal policy and spending priorities (Section 202 [f] [1];

—to provide the Budget Committees with other such analyses of federal policy, as the CBO sees fit (Section 202 [f] [2]).

Budget analysis—the computation of spending and tax estimates—was the CBO's bread and butter. The budget process could survive without the CBO's analysis of the pros and cons of federal policies, but it hardly could operate if Congress could not compute how much the government's programs were going to cost. Never before had Congress been able to challenge the spending and tax estimates of the executive branch. The new CBO, like the president's Office of Management and Budget, had to rely on the executive departments and agencies for the basic data about what the government was doing. But the CBO could make different assumptions from the OMB's about the way federal programs would operate; for example, it could make its own estimates of how many college students would qualify for federal aid and how fast the states would spend federal grants for sewer construction. Sometimes the CBO's estimates proved closer to the truth than those of the executive branch, and sometimes they did not. But in any case, the CBO provided Congress with budget estimates free of the political considerations that often colored the estimates of the executive branch. The OMB, to discourage support of a program the president did not like, might estimate its costs higher than were probable. Or, to make the president's proposed deficit look artificially low, the

OMB might predict unrealistically large receipts from federal taxes and services. The CBO often blew the whistle on these kinds of practices. "OMB doesn't fudge as much by choosing numbers that help them," said James L. Blum, the assistant CBO director for budget analysis. "We're all a lot more careful now that there's competition."[24]

Generating budget estimates proved to be an enormous task, much more time-consuming than the CBO at first had expected. When Rivlin requested a staff of 259 persons in 1975, she made room for fifty-one staffers in the budget analysis division. Two years later, even though Congress had limited her staff to 208, budget analysis had a staff of sixty-seven. The redeployment meant that the CBO had to transfer seven staffers to budget analysis from other divisions and dismiss another three members of the other divisions' support staffs. Even so, the Budget Committee staffs felt that the CBO should devote still more of its staff to budget analysis.[25] Computers, vital to the CBO's budget analysis, cost about $2 million a year—or 20 percent of the CBO's budget. Rivlin regarded the establishment of the CBO's computerized scorekeeping system as one of the office's most important accomplishments in its early years.[26]

The House Commission on Information and Facilities gave the CBO high marks for the budget estimates that it provided to Congress. It sent a questionnaire to the staffs of the congressional committees that formed the clientele for the CBO's budget analysis. Table 3 shows the result.[27] For the House and Senate Budget Committees, one of the CBO's most important tasks was scorekeeping—computing whether legislation enacted by Congress was consistent with its most recent budget resolution. Neither Budget Committee had any serious complaints about the accuracy and timeliness of the CBO's scorekeeping. As might be expected, the Senate Budget Committee made more use of the CBO's scorekeeping than the House committee, which developed the capacity to do much of the work itself.[28] However, the House Budget

Table 3   *Congressional Committee Staffs Rate the CBO*

	Number of Responses		
	Favorable	*Neutral*	*Unfavorable*
Scorekeeping	19	3	4
Projections of the impact of spending and tax bills	11	4	4
Five-year projections of the entire budget	10	9	5
Accuracy of projections of the impact of authorizing bills	14	3	2
Timeliness of projections of the impact of authorizing bills	16	2	1

Source: House Commission on Information and Facilities

Committee used the CBO's scorekeeping system, if not the numbers themselves, to record committee decisions on budget resolutions and to allocate resolutions' spending totals among House committees with jurisdiction over spending legislation. The Senate Budget Committee used another CBO product, its annual five-year projection of the costs of maintaining current federal programs, as the basis for its markup of its annual first budget resolution. The Budget Committees found the CBO's budget analysis seriously deficient in only one respect: its failure to predict or even to explain the outlay shortfall that baffled the executive branch as well as Congress during the mid-1970s. In the 1976 and 1977 fiscal years, outlays fell billions of dollars short of estimates made by both the OMB and the CBO. The CBO, lacking a capacity to examine outlay trends during the course of a fiscal year, left itself powerless to determine the causes. But if it was any consolation, the OMB also was at a loss to explain the shortfalls.

The House and Senate Appropriations Committees, with experienced staffs that had grown set in their ways, made little use of the CBO's budget analysis. For the Appropriations Committees, the budget reform act required the CBO to perform only one major service—an estimate of the outlay effect over five years of the budget authority included in each appropriations bill. The CBO performed the task as required, but the Appropriations Committees could hardly have cared less; they thought in terms of budget authority, not outlays. "It's just a burdensome reporting requirement," said one House Appropriations Committee staff member.[29] The CBO might have helped the Appropriations Committees estimate budget authority for the many uncontrollable programs, such as food stamps, for which they had no choice but to provide sufficient funds. But instead, the Appropriations Committees relied largely on the executive branch, as their staff members had done for years. The CBO found the Appropriations Committees too set in their ways to listen to a new source of budget information.[30] However, a staff member of the House Appropriations Subcommittee on Defense said he found the CBO too busy with its other tasks to provide the subcommittee with estimates in the form in which it needed them.[31]

The CBO's most time-consuming job under the budget reform act was the projection over five years of the impact of every authorizing bill reported by a congressional committee. The CBO did not try to meet this requirement in 1975, when it was still getting organized. In 1976, the CBO estimated the cost of 282 authorizing bills, or 44 percent of those reported.[32] In the early months of 1977, its batting average improved to 64 percent.[33] Most authorizing committees had never estimated the cost of the bills they reported. In some cases they did not want Congress to know how expensive their legislation might be, lest high spending totals frighten potential supporters. In others, authorizing committees were simply not aware that the CBO was available to help them determine the cost of their legislation. Early in 1976, the CBO staff, assisted by the Budget Committee staffs, had to keep a close watch on the authorizing committees as they prepared legislation. But as the months wore on, the authorizing committees became more aware of—and less hostile toward—the CBO. They increasingly took the initiative to notify the CBO of legislation under preparation, as reflected in the growing percentage of authorizing bills for which the CBO provided cost estimates. The Senate Veterans' Affairs Committee found the CBO to be "an effective counterweight to outrageous cost estimates of the Veterans Administration. It used to be that we were at the mercy of the people who operated the computers for the executive branch."[34]

The clients least effectively served by the CBO were the tax committees—House Ways and Means and Senate Finance. The budget reform act required the CBO to estimate federal revenue and tax expenditures on most occasions when it also had to provide Congress with projections of total spending. However, the staff of the Joint Committee on Internal Revenue Taxation (the joint committee's membership was identical to that of the Ways and Means and Finance Committees) already prepared that kind of information. Early in the CBO's existence, the joint committee's staff warned the CBO not to try to horn in. Accordingly, the CBO relied on the joint committee staff for most projections of total revenue. It omitted revenue from the fiscal 1978 version of its annual five-year projection of the budget, because the joint committee staff did not provide it with one.[35] The CBO's tax policy division proved more useful in defining and estimating tax expenditures, which the joint committee staff had not studied closely. However, the chief clients for the CBO's tax expenditure work were not the tax committees but the Budget Committees. For example, the CBO helped the Senate Budget Committee staff in 1976 to write one of the most comprehensive studies to date on tax reform.[36]

While it reduced congressional dependence on the executive branch, the budget analysis supplied by the CBO did not often have a direct impact on policy. But occasionally it influenced the outcome of a particular policy debate. For example, the House in 1976 considered a bill[37] that would have provided federal pensions for coal miners with twenty-five or thirty years of experience in the mines. The Ford administration, which opposed the legislation, estimated its annual cost at $700 million. The CBO, on the other hand, estimated an annual cost of less than $200 million. The House Education and Labor Subcommittee on Labor Standards tightened the language of the bill to ensure that the assumptions made by the administration in its $700 million estimate were false. The bill eventually cleared the House but not the Senate.

The CBO's estimates did not always support its clients' policy positions. In 1976, President Ford vetoed legislation[38] that would have increased the federal price support level for milk. The administration estimated that the bill would cost $540 million over five years. Using different assumptions about the supply of milk in coming years, the House Agriculture Committee, which supported the bill, made a much lower cost estimate. The CBO judged that the administration's estimate was closer. The Agriculture Committee complained that the CBO was a shill for the administration. But in the Senate, Muskie and Bellmon, the leaders of the Budget Committee, accepted the CBO's figures and supported the veto. The Senate failed by a large margin to override the veto.[39]

POLICY ANALYSIS

Vital as it was to the day-to-day operation of the budget process, budget analysis was not what attracted Rivlin to the Congressional Budget Office. Budget analysis—or "numbers crunching," as it was known in the budget business—was mostly a routine chore, not likely to appeal to a veteran of a think tank like the Brookings Institution. Rivlin joined the CBO to perform policy analysis—to evaluate the pros and cons of alternative courses of federal policy. Muskie promised her when he secured her appointment to the CBO that she would be given the time and resources to do policy analysis not only in response to specific congressional requests but also at her own initiative, consistent with the budget reform act's provision that the CBO supply Congress with analytical reports "as may be necessary or appropriate."[40] The House

Appropriations Subcommittee on the Legislative Branch entertained a proposal in 1975 to abolish the CBO's policy analysis capability. When the proposal failed, Rivlin was left free to pursue policy analysis.

Rivlin intentionally isolated her policy analysts from the CBO's budget analysis division. She feared that if policy and budget analysis were combined, the policy analysts would find themselves so caught up in the day-to-day tasks of computing budget estimates that they would not have time to prepare thoughtful studies of federal policy alternatives. For this decision she took much criticism from both Budget Committees, which maintained that budget analysis and policy analysis overlapped. Indeed, the CBO's budget analysts had to be familiar with the nature of the programs they examined, while the policy analysts had to know the costs of various program alternatives. But Rivlin held firm, organizing most of her policy analysts into three CBO divisions that covered the spectrum of federal spending programs: one for human resources and community development, one for natural resources and commerce, and one for national security and international affairs. In addition, she established a fiscal analysis division to prepare economic studies.

Many of the policy studies turned out by the CBO were of extremely high quality, superior to the comparable products of the other congressional support offices and most executive branch agencies. "I would give those I have read a very high average grade," wrote William Capron of Harvard University. "None of the formal reports I have examined are shoddy or biased; most are highly credible and knowledgeable, and a few are, in my view, outstanding."[41] Even Rep. Jack Brooks, one of the leading critics of the CBO's penchant for publicity, found that the CBO offered Congress "increasingly skilled analytical support."[42]

But the CBO's policy studies had one major defect: Congress did not use them very much. Responsibility lay in part with those members of Congress who preferred to rely on their own political instincts for their decisions on policy. As Muskie said, "The very conservative senators would rather see no analysis at all."[43] Some of the fault rested with congressional committee staffs, which did not always like to admit that the CBO could perform policy analysis superior to their own. But the CBO itself had to accept a good share of the blame. It published some of its studies too late; an analysis of welfare reform, a year in the making, came out in the summer of 1977, after the Carter administration and the relevant congressional committees had prepared their positions. Other CBO studies failed to define issues in terms that Congress found useful; an analysis of higher education programs did not treat benefits available under the GI bill or social security. At a time when the economy was such a dominant issue, only the fiscal analysis division could be depended upon to produce studies that would attract wide attention on Capitol Hill.

The CBO's major piece of policy analysis—its annual report on budget options, to be submitted to the Budget Committees by April 1—was, ironically, one of its poorest. In 1975, Rivlin was appointed CBO director barely a month before the annual report was due, and she did not try to produce one. Instead, the Budget Committees enlisted a group of outside budget experts led by Samuel Cohn, a former assistant OMB director, to prepare a scaled-down version of an annual report. Cohn submitted the report[44] on April 15, too late to help the Budget Committees, which had already reported their first budget resolutions for fiscal 1976. The CBO proper wrote its first annual report in 1976. It set a target completion date in February, more than a month ahead of the budget reform act's deadline, but Budget Committee criticism of an early draft forced the CBO to rewrite it and delayed publication until March 15. Even in rewritten form, the 392-page report[45] proved of little value to the Budget Committees in their markups of the first budget resolution for fiscal 1977. In seeking to analyze the entire budget, the CBO had failed to achieve the sophistication and depth that the

Budget Committees needed. The committees complained, for example, that the report merely listed several possible sizes for the Navy's fleet, without analyzing the costs and benefits of each.

Rivlin revamped the annual report in 1977, reducing it to 202 pages and supporting it with twenty-eight separate publications analyzing specific budget issues. One section of the annual report itself,[46] a description of the difficulty facing President Carter as he sought his goal of a balanced budget by fiscal 1981, received considerable attention both on Capitol Hill and in the press, as did some of the twenty-eight budget issue papers. The package had more impact on the upcoming budget resolution than the annual report of the previous year, but that wasn't saying much. The Senate Budget Committee, in material prepared for the committee members' use during markup, referred to the CBO report exactly once, in its discussion of defense manpower. In addition, Senate Budget Committee staff members said their expositions of some other issues were influenced by the CBO. The House Budget Committee ignored the CBO report.

Some of the CBO's individual pieces of policy analysis—both those that were background papers for the fiscal 1978 annual report and those that were independent—proved more useful to Congress, especially the Senate. The House, a large body of 435 members who specialized in individual federal programs, was uninterested in the CBO's policy analysis role from the beginning. But the hundred senators did not have so much time to specialize; they were more likely clients for the CBO's studies of broad federal policy issues. In practice, the CBO's formal studies did not have so much impact as the informal discussions between the CBO and congressional staffs preliminary to publication of the studies. Publication was designed more than anything else to lift the morale of the CBO policy analysts; the CBO staff members, unlike most governmental staffers, had their own names, not those of their supervisers, attached to their reports. The CBO policy analysts who had the most impact on legislation were those who fed information to congressional committees during preparation of their studies. "You don't wait until you have the product to sell it," said C. William Fischer, the CBO's first assistant director for human resources and community development. "You get the customer involved in the development."[47]

G. William Hoagland, an analyst on Fischer's staff, was one of the more successful practitioners of this strategy. A former budget analyst for the Agriculture Department, Hoagland in 1975 became a CBO policy analyst with considerable experience in budget estimating. As it happened, the CBO's budget analyst for welfare programs was overworked in 1975, and Hoagland helped him by preparing budget estimates for the food stamp program, a welfare program run by the Agriculture Department. As Rivlin had feared, Hoagland's activities as a budget estimator cut into the time available for his central job—policy analysis. But they helped him gain the acquaintance and the confidence of the House and Senate Agriculture Committee staffs. Although budget estimating occupied a good deal of his time, Hoagland still was able to gather material for an excellent 1977 policy study of food stamps.[48] The published study, which analyzed the consequences of maintaining the food stamp program or changing it in any of four ways, was too late to influence the 1976 debate over the program. But the Agriculture Committees used Hoagland's information as he accumulated it and shared it with them. Indeed, The Senate Agriculture Committee invited Hoagland to advise it during its markup of 1976 food stamp legislation.

The natural resources and commerce division followed the reverse strategy, generally with less success. The policy analysts in that division avoided day-to-day contacts with congressional staff members and instead concentrated on exhaustive studies that might, by virtue of their quality alone, gain the attention of committee staffs. While their analyses did not always have the intended effect, some of them entered the congressional debate. For example, one 1975 CBO report dealt with commercialization of synthetic fuel development, an issue that divided the House and Senate during debate of a bill authorizing funds for the Energy Research and Development Administration. The Senate amended the bill with a provision of federal guarantees for up to $6 billion in loans to businesses that undertook synthetic fuel development. House opponents of this provision used the CBO report to bolster their position.[49] Senators who supported the loan guarantees were angry with the CBO for supplying ammunition to the opposition.[50] The House prevailed, knocking the loan guarantees out of the conference report on the bill.[51] The entire episode proved somewhat embarrassing to Rivlin, who felt that the CBO's reputation for impartiality suffered. She maintained that the CBO report "does not contain any specific recommendations . . . but merely represents an effort to begin sorting out in a thoughtful manner some of the issues in this complex field."[52]

PROSPECTS

If the Congressional Budget Office's early performance is any indication, embarrassments of this kind are likely to continue as long as the CBO has an active director who seeks to make an impact on the congressional decision-making process. Congress will have to learn to live with a CBO whose analyses bolster the arguments of one side of policy debates. If that is too great a price to pay, Congress will lose its source of independent budgetary information.

As Sen. Sam Ervin, one of the fathers of budget reform, told the Senate in 1974, "One of the main factors for the unfortunate mismatch in budget power between the legislative and executive branches has been the superior informational resources of the president and executive agencies and the inability of Congress to obtain information which would enable it to take an independent position."[53] The CBO helped Congress obtain the information that began to set it free.

CHAPTER 7

SHAPING CONGRESSIONAL POLICY

BUDGET REFORM WAS a procedural reform; it should not necessarily have affected policy in any particular way. If it had been calculated to serve the interests of the liberals or the conservatives, it never could have been enacted with only token opposition. But it would be a hollow process indeed that did not affect policy at all. If Congress enacted the same legislation with the new budget process as it would have enacted without it, why should it bother with the complicated procedures at all? If a rational and coherent structure for making decisions led to the same results as a random and haphazard one, who needed rationality and coherence?

The first few years of experience provided no conclusive verdict on budget reform's impact. On the one hand, congressional liberals and conservatives, who had hoped for substantial changes in the budget, were both disappointed. Liberals had wanted to overturn the spending priorities of the president, especially while a Republican lived in the White House. Conservatives had seen an opportunity to cut federal spending and reduce the deficit. Neither was satisfied. On a grand scale, the new budget process caused hardly more than a ripple on the vast surface of the federal budget. Federal spending kept growing after 1974 about as fast as it had before. The deficit, greater than $40 billion in the last year before the new process took effect, grew even larger in the next three years. Spending priorities might have begun a new long-term trend; defense spending, whose share of federal outlays had been declining since its Vietnam War peak, leveled off after 1974. But this very likely would have happened whether there had been budget reform or not.

However, it would be wrong to conclude that the new process amounted to nothing more than a complicated exercise in arithmetic. The introduction of the budget process changed the complexion of congressional politics. Conservatives realized that they had to live with huge deficits during times of high unemployment. Liberals backed off from pushing costly new programs for fear of besmirching Congress's incipient reputation for fiscal responsibility.

In many small ways, the budget process changed the nature of congressional decisions. Its mere existence created a counterpoint to the demands of special interest groups and permitted the enactment of economy measures in government pensions and highway construction. It changed the shape of the 1976 tax bill. It helped Congress override vetoes of legislation that was consistent with the congressional budget even though it violated the president's.

CONTROLLING THE BUDGET

That the more ambitious of liberals and conservatives would be disappointed by the results of the budget process was predictable. As a practical matter, the possibilities of quick, dramatic changes in the size or the shape of the budget are severely limited. According to the Office of Management and Budget, 75 percent of all outlays in each coming fiscal year were automatic—they were difficult or impossible to change—in the mid-1970s.[1] Congress could do nothing about interest payments on the national debt, which soaked up 10 percent of the budget. It could not stop payments for social security and other entitlement programs, which cost nearly $175 billion in the first year of the new budget process. It could not renege on contracts ($50 billion) without incurring penalties.

Circumstances beyond congressional control regularly caused major swings in the uncontrollable part of the budget, much to the frustration of Congress. For example, every increase of one percentage point in the unemployment rate cost the government some $16 billion through reduced income tax receipts and increased outlays for welfare and unemployment benefits. Even when economic conditions did not fluctuate, the Office of Management and Budget was unable to estimate outlays accurately. Spending underruns of billions of dollars developed in the 1976 and 1977 fiscal years for reasons that OMB was unable to isolate. Its fiscal 1977 outlay estimate fell by $6 billion between February and April of 1977.[2]

Even the controllable 25 percent of the budget included expenditures, such as military salaries, that Congress could not realistically hope to change significantly in a short period of time. The Brookings Institution estimated that of the $366 billion budget for fiscal 1976, Congress actually could cut no more than $6 billion to $11 billion.[3] If it was to wield significant influence over the rest of the budget, Congress needed to look beyond the coming year to the future, when the pieces of the budget could be manipulated more effectively. But the Budget Committees found the day-to-day operation of the new budget process enough of a challenge in their early years, and they did not pay much attention to the long term.

Forced to deal with a budget whose shape was largely predetermined, the Budget Committees used budget resolutions mostly to predict spending and revenue for the coming year. For spending programs over which Congress could exercise discretion, they usually tried to set targets high enough so that they would not impinge severely on other committees' plans. While a presidential budget embodies the philosophy of one man, a congressional budget must be acceptable to a majority of 535 men and women whose views span the political spectrum, and it can contain nothing violently objectionable to significant groups. Thus, for example, Adams supported small sums in the first budget resolution for fiscal 1977 for start-up costs for national health insurance and full employment legislation. He said the committees responsible for this legislation "should have an opportunity to come to the floor without somebody saying, 'No, you can't even consider starting up such a program.' "[4]

A second factor, inherent in the nature of budget resolutions, reduced their potential to shape the spending side of the budget. The budget reform act provided that spending be divided among the sixteen functions of the federal government. It would have been more efficient to divide the resolution among actual spending bills—so much for food stamps, so much for the public works appropriations bill, and so on. But the Appropriations Committees and other committees with responsibility for spending legislation would not have tolerated a budget process that told them exactly what they could and could not do. So Congressman Bolling hit upon the division of spending by function as a way to set priorities without trampling on the jurisdiction of the spending committees. The trouble was that the functions did not mean much to most senators and representatives, because spending legislation was organized around programs, not functions. The appropriations bill for the Department of Housing and Urban Development and related agencies provided funds for programs that fell into twelve of the sixteen functions. Responsibility for funding the natural resources, environment, and energy function was divided among seven of the regular appropriations bills and countless backdoor spending bills.

In the first year of the new budget process, it was virtually impossible to figure out what the budget resolutions meant for each spending bill. The Budget Committees did not translate the functional breakdown of spending into the amount of spending in the jurisdiction of each other committee, as they would be required to do in future years. The House Budget Committee informally estimated the size of each piece of spending legislation that would be necessary to achieve the targets of the first resolution. The Senate Budget Committee, not wishing to appear to be dictating the size of each spending bill, did nothing comparable. The result sometimes was comic and confused. When Senator McClellan, chairman of the Senate Appropriations Committee, wanted to know whether the fiscal 1976 appropriations bill for the Labor and HEW Departments exceeded the targets of the first budget resolution, he could not get a straight answer. Here is a condensed version of his exchange with Muskie:

> McCLELLAN: Why did the Committee on the Budget find it necessary to make the process so confusing? I do not understand how it works. Why could the committee not follow the appropriation bill so its analysis would be simple, understandable, and we would all know what we are doing and what we are expected to do?
>
> MUSKIE: It is not quite that black and white.
>
> McCLELLAN: Well, now, that gets more confusion. Why—if we are given a certain amount for these functions—when we total them up, can we not tell whether this bill exceeds the congressional budget resolution?
>
> MUSKIE: My speech is in answer to that question.
>
> McCLELLAN: I would like to have a yes or no answer to my question.
>
> MUSKIE: One of the reasons the senator is confused is because too many people have looked for simple answers to a very complex problem.
>
> McCLELLAN: I asked only a simple question whether this bill exceeds the concurrent resolution. I do not know why it takes a half-hour's speech to answer it.[5]

Muskie never gave the simple answer that McClellan wanted. Instead, he said the bill exceeded the targets for three of the functions for which it appropriated funds and fell short of the targets for three other functions. He also warned that McClellan's bill combined with other legislation then in preparation in the Senate might carry spending over the targets in the other three functions.

After the first year, confusion was moderated by the required allocation of the first resolution's spending targets among congressional committees responsible for legislation providing funds for programs. In addition, the Appropriations Committees had to divide their totals among their thirteen subcommittees, each of which then had a target to aim at. But there was still a catch. Many appropriations bills had to leave out funds for one or more programs whose authorizing legislation had not been enacted at the time that the appropriations bills moved through Congress. For example, the fiscal 1977 Labor–HEW appropriations bill had to omit funds for a variety of health and education programs scheduled to expire at the end of fiscal 1976 and not yet reauthorized. The House Budget Committee, whose first goal in these circumstances was to avoid confusion, computed how much spending the rest of the bill should contain. But the Senate Budget Committee, still unwilling to appear to be setting spending targets for individual programs, did not, and the Senate Appropriations Committee was unable to tell precisely how its Labor–HEW bill compared with its spending targets.

THE BUDGET PROCESS AND TAXES

If obstacles stood in the way of using budget resolutions to shape the spending side of the budget, resolutions were even weaker on the revenue side. Where spending was divided among the sixteen functions, revenue appeared as a single number—a grand total. Budget Committee reports accompanying resolutions were to divide the revenue total among "the major sources of such revenues"—personal income tax, social security tax, and the like.[6] But report language was far less influential on Congress than the resolution itself, because

Congress voted only on the resolution, not on the report. In its report for the first budget resolution for fiscal 1977, the Senate Budget Committee included a reduction in tax expenditures as a source of $2 billion in revenue.[7] Muskie tried to enforce that provision when the Senate took up the 1976 tax bill. His effort developed into a summer-long struggle with Finance Committee chairman Russell Long, who came out the winner on the Senate floor.

Tax expenditures are special provisions of the tax code that allow tax relief to encourage certain kinds of economic activity or to benefit taxpayers in special circumstances. For example, the tax credit for business investment is designed to provide an incentive for business expansion, while the exclusion of social security benefits from taxable income provides aid for the elderly. Most tax expenditures are equivalent to direct spending programs. The business investment tax credit is the same as a federal grant program for businesses that invest their profits in expansion, and the social security exclusion is equivalent to additional benefits for the elderly. Most tax expenditures can be classified by budget function, just as spending can. The business investment tax credit belongs in the commerce and transportation function, while the social security exclusion serves the purpose of providing income security.

However, the budget reform act did not treat tax expenditures as the equivalent of direct spending programs. It required the Budget Committees to list tax expenditures by function in their reports accompanying first budget resolutions—but not in the resolutions themselves.[8] Thus the budget process did not present Congress with an opportunity to look at tax expenditures and direct spending together as it set priorities. Congress did not regard the business investment tax credit as a form of federal aid to business, nor did it include the social security exclusion as aid to the elderly. Because they were treated as offsets to receipts, tax expenditures simply got lost in the grand total for revenue. That meant that Congress ignored $103 billion worth of federal activity—the equivalent of 25 percent of direct outlays—as it set federal spending priorities for fiscal 1977.[9]

The Senate Government Operations Committee's version of the budget reform act would have required Congress to give equal treatment to spending tax expenditures. But the Senate Finance Committee did not want budget reform to interfere with its freedom to write tax legislation. Its staff, active in the effort led by the Rules and Administration Committee to rewrite the Government Operations Committee's bill, was instrumental in dropping equivalency for tax expenditures from the final Senate version of the bill. Moreover, the concept of tax expenditures was not well developed in 1974. Tax expenditures had not even been compiled into a single list until 1969, and they were not subject to the same rigorous analysis as spending programs.[10] The budget reform act, while not going as far as the Senate Government Operations Committee would have liked, nevertheless raised tax expenditures to a new level of congressional awareness.

FISCAL POLICY

Because the shaky economy was the top political issue of the day, fiscal policy dominated the budget debate during budget reform's first years. As it was supposed to, the budget process focused congressional attention on the important totals—spending, revenue, the deficit. "No longer can we consider each spending program singularly, with no awareness or concern of its effect on the total level of federal spending," said Sen. Henry Bellmon. "Our decision-making process should now be informed and deliberate."[11]

When the Senate Budget Committee prepared the very first congressional budget resolution in 1975, Muskie separated from the rest of the budget a set of proposals designed to accelerate economic recover. Perhaps no other committee with legislative authority had ever before focused on the amount of stimulus the economy needed from the federal government.

Impact on fiscal policy became an important ingredient in congressional tax debates, even though the budget process was geared less toward taxes than toward spending. When the Senate took up the 1976 tax bill, the economic impact of proposals to create or eliminate tax expenditures became as important as the tax expenditures' intrinsic merit. In the following year, fiscal policy influenced the fate of proposals to shore up the social security system by increasing the social security tax. Congress rejected an immediate tax increase, partly out of concern that it would retard the growth of an already sluggish economy.

But it was on the spending side of the budget that fiscal policy considerations had their greatest impact. By keeping Congress painfully aware of the deficit, the budget process discouraged new spending. The reasons were more political than economic: senators and representatives did not want to appear to their constituents to be responsible for any more red ink. Muskie, who had worked so hard when the budget reform act was written to keep it from automatically serving the cause of fiscal conservatives, became the first to boast of its capacity to discourage spending. In the summer of 1976, he said the new process would hold spending $15 billion lower in fiscal 1977 than it otherwise would have reached.[12] A few months later, he went even further: "Had it not been for the congressional budget process, federal spending and the federal deficit for the two years during which we have been operating under the congressional budget would have been higher by a range of at least $15 billion to $30 billion."[13] That's probably an exaggeration, although there is no way to prove or disprove it. However, it is clear that the budget process had an impact on individual spending bills.

Occasionally, the Budget Committees made themselves felt by putting pressure on Congress to cut spending bills as they moved through the House and Senate. The Senate Budget Committee went to the Senate floor to force small reductions in the 1975 military procurement and school lunch bills. Both Muskie and Giaimo tried to reduce the size of the 1977 farm bill. They failed—but at least they forced Congress to recognize the impact of the bill on the already enormous fiscal 1978 deficit.

Congressional committees sometimes may have reported somewhat smaller spending bills than they would have without the presence of the budget process. Before sending legislation to the floor, committee chairmen frequently checked with the Budget Committees to determine whether it was consistent with the most recent budget resolution. The Senate Agriculture Committee invited a Budget Committee staff member to attend its markup of 1976 food stamp legislation to keep it in line with the congressional budget. The House Budget Committee wielded most of its influence at a committee-to-committee level. In 1977, for example, the House Education and Labor Committee reported a bill that would have allowed more generous benefits than were included in the first budget resolution for fiscal 1978 for coal miners suffering from black lung disease. The House Budget Committee brought that fact to the attention of the Education and Labor Committee, which scaled down the benefits accordingly.

On other occasions, the Budget Committees played a different kind of role—as catalysts for the enactment of certain economy measures. The committees were critical to the effort to repeal the 1-percent kicker—the bonus that retired federal workers enjoyed in their pension benefits. The House Budget Committee played a vital role when Congress placed an outlay ceiling for fiscal 1977 on highway construction—although, as it turned out, states did not build enough highways that year to reach the ceiling. The year before, Muskie's support was important to the successful effort to limit federal pay raised to 5 percent instead of 8.66 percent.

In all these cases, the Budget Committees served as counterweights to the special interests that sought federal benefits.

The special interests had cozy relationships with the committees responsible for their legislation. Groups of retired federal employees had many friends on the Post Office and Civil Service Committees, and the Public Works Committees listened carefully to the highway lobby. But the Budget Committees had to manage the entire federal budget, not just the pieces that affected particular interest groups. They were in a position to say there was no room in the congressional budget for an individual spending program, no matter how meritorious it might seem to a special interest group. Sometimes the Budget Committees succumbed to interest group pressure, as when the House Budget Committee reversed its decision in 1976 to reduce the federal subsidy for lower-class mail. But on many occasions, their role paralleled that of the Office of Management and Budget in the executive branch. Just as OMB required executive departments and agencies to economize, the Budget Committees forced economy measures on other congressional committees.

Despite the bias toward spending restraint during a time of huge deficits, the budget process discouraged across-the-board spending cuts, the indiscriminate approach to thrift in government that Congress had taken in the late 1960s. After the Senate Budget Committee set spending targets for the sixteen budget functions in the first budget resolution for fiscal 1976, Sen. Ernest F. Hollings proposed that the committee reduce the spending total by $3.6 billion by cutting 1 percent from each function. But Sen. Lawton Chiles, who had supported such efforts in the past, said that to adopt Hollings's proposal would be to "surrender our prerogatives and responsibilities" to determine the shape of federal spending. Added Sen. J. Glenn Beall, "If after having gone through this process, we are forced to take meat-ax percentage cuts in a proposed budget, then we really have not done our job." The committee defeated Hollings's proposal 11-3.[14]

Congressional understanding of fiscal policy grew perceptibly with the introduction of budget reform. In particular, the budget process helped Congress realize that it was helpless to hold the annual deficit much below the $50 billion to $70 billion range during periods of economic weakness. When it was proposed in the Senate that outlays in the first budget resolution for fiscal 1976 be cut by $25 billion to reduce the deficit, Senator Beall, although a fiscal conservative, offered a sophisticated rebuttal: such a massive spending cut would reverse the economic recovery, cutting tax revenue, increasing welfare spending, and leaving the deficit no lower than it had been.[15] In the House, the most conservative Republicans offered budget resolution amendments in the first two years of budget reform that would have balanced the budget—at least on paper. But by 1977, the conservatives, recognizing the unlikelihood of balancing the budget, instead proposed huge spending cuts accompanied by tax cuts that would stimulate the economy and bring relief to taxpayers.

TARGETS AND CEILINGS

The degree of spending restraint imposed by the budget process, though too small to satisfy conservatives, was due in part to the mistaken belief that the first budget resolution set spending ceilings, not targets. Congressional committees, encouraged by the Budget Committee chairmen—especially Muskie—labored to hold their legislation below the targets of the first resolution. It was as if the resolution's spending total was a bull's-eye at the top of an archery target instead of in the center. Points were scored if the arrow landed below the bull's-eye, as long as it hit the target. But it was a complete miss if the arrow was just too high for the bull's-eye and sailed past the target.

Muskie regularly interpreted the targets as ceilings when he wanted to use them to restrain spending. In debate of the 1975 school lunch bill, he said:

> We still reached a ceiling because we were required to do so by law. Now we have to make the process of adhering to that ceiling one of deliberate decision making.[16]

Adams, unwilling to appear to be restraining the spending instincts of other committees, took care not to make the targets more powerful than the budget reform act intended them to be. As he told the House:

> Appropriations and other spending bills—as well as revenue measures—may exceed or fall short of the targets without violating either the letter or the spirit of the budget process.[17]

But that was not always the message that particular committee chairmen received. Adams as well as Muskie frequently praised other committees for keeping their spending legislation within—that is, at or below—the targets. Here is Adams on the fiscal 1977 appropriations bill for the Treasury Department:

> The appropriations in this bill as reported by the Appropriations Committee are well within the amounts assumed in the first concurrent resolution on the budget.[18]

Rep. Tom Steed, chairman of the subcommittee that prepared the legislation, got the message: ". . . this particular bill will be well within the limit set by the Committee on the Budget."[19] Similarly, when Muskie said the fiscal 1977 appropriations bill for the Labor and Health, Education and Welfare Departments was "well within the subcommitttee's allocation," Sen. Warren G. Magnuson, chairman of the Labor-HEW subcommittee, said: "This bill is still under the budget ceiling."[20]

Like Steed and Magnuson, most committee and subcommittee chairmen viewed their budget resolution allocations as maximums. The Budget Committee chairmen—again, especially Muskie—took it as a measure of success when actual spending proved less than was included in budget resolutions. In early 1977, projected outlays for fiscal 1977 were $410 billion, short of the $413 billion in both the first and second budget resolutions for that year. "If we can project $413 billion and spend only $410 billion," Muskie said, "that's the best evidence the public can have that the budget process is working."[21]

SPENDING PRIORITIES

Spending shortfalls of this kind had no serious impact on the fiscal policy of the congressional budget. For example, the fiscal 1976 deficit turned out to be about $2 billion less than the target of the first resolution and nearly $8 billion under the ceiling of the second. But even $8 billion is not a lot in an economy of $1.6 trillion.

However, shortfalls could severely distort congressional spending priorities when they were concentrated in particular budget functions. For example, the first resolution for fiscal 1976 made room for $28.5 billion in outlays for two of the budget functions that included many of the federal jobs programs.[22] Actual outlays turned out to be just $23.5 billion, a decrease of 18 percent. At the same time, defense spending, targeted at $90.7 billion in the first resolution, fell only $700 million short. Thus spending in the two domestic functions, targeted at 31 percent of defense outlays in the first resolution, proved to be just 26 percent. Likewise, budget authority provided by Congress in 1976 for the two domestic functions fell from 30 percent of defense in the first resolution to 26 percent in reality.

Adams at least showed an understanding that congressional spending priorities were at stake when Congress had to decide whether spending legislation should reach up to the targets. He told the House:

> When we establish general targets in the first resolution, we should support congressional efforts to maintain spending efforts within those targets as well as supporting efforts to reduce spending when targets are exceeded.[23]

But Muskie's concern for spending restraint outweighed his desire to maintain congressional spending priorities. He remarked during a committee meeting:

If we come to regard budget resolutions as mandates for spending, that would change the whole nature of the process. If we come in below the ceilings, that's fine with me.[24]

Only one circumstance—the presidential veto—propelled the Budget Committees into a defense of congressional spending priorities. In 1975, Congress handily overrode President Ford's veto of the fiscal 1976 education appropriations bill, which exceeded the president's budget request but not the congressional budget resolution.[25] It easily enacted over Ford's veto the school lunch bill that the Senate Budget Committee had helped cut back before it cleared the Senate.[26] In 1976, Congress failed once, despite the Budget Committees' best efforts, to override a veto of a public works bill that included the authorization of countercyclical revenue sharing, one of Muskie's favorite programs. Congress trimmed the program later in the year and enacted it over another veto.[27]

The Budget Committees' half-hearted defense of congressional spending priorities was consistent with their lukewarm concern for priorities during preparation of budget resolutions. The committees were so absorbed by the problems of the economy that they had little time to consider whether, for example, a spending cut in defense was too great a price to pay for national health insurance. "I would have expected some discussion of these kinds of issues," said CBO director Rivlin, "but so far there hasn't been very much."[28] To be sure, Budget Committee Democrats worked for cuts from President Ford's defense budgets and increases to his requests for domestic programs. The debate over the appropriate level of defense spending grew intense when the House Budget Committee tried to cut the fiscal 1978 defense budget of President Carter. But on the whole, the Budget Committees did not take advantage of the opportunity to weigh one budget function against another. Instead, they prepared their budget resolutions by working through the budget one function at a time.

When budget resolutions went to the House and Senate floors, it was a rare occasion when a senator or a representative tried to increase spending for one function at the expense of another. In the Senate, leaders of both parties opposed amendments of any kind on the floor. Resolutions sailed through the Senate floor unamended until 1977, when funds were added to the first resolution for fiscal 1978 for housing, community development, and veterans benefits. In the House, Congresswoman Holtzman offered an amendment to the first resolution for fiscal 1977 that would have transferred $7.5 billion in budget authority from defense to "desperately needed programs here in the United States," including crime fighting, medical research, job training, and college aid. But Holtzman, regarded by her fellow House members as a fringe liberal, failed to trigger much of a debate with her proposal, which was defeated 317 to 85.[29] A year later, Rep. Parren Mitchell offered a similar amendment for $6.5 billion. After perfunctory debate, the House voted down his amendment, 306 to 102.[30] More typical were amendments on the House floor to add small amounts of budget authority for particular programs, amounts as small as $15 million to audit tax returns in fiscal 1977. Proposals of this nature were designed to make room in the resolution for the sponsor's favorite program—not to set off any serious debate.

If conservatives were dissatisfied over the failure of the budget process to slash the deficit, it was the liberals who were most disappointed with its failure to force Congress to come to grips with spending priorities. "I am deeply disturbed," said Holtzman, "that the budget we are presented with this time fails to carry out the essential promise of the budget act—to set congresssional priorities."[31] Rep. James G. O'Hara, another liberal House Budget Committee member, said after the conclusion of the first year of budget reform, "We should have produced a true Democratic alternative to the administration's conservative approach—and we haven't."[32] The Council on National Priorities and Resources, which was formed in 1973 to fight President Nixon's proposed cuts in domestic programs, lobbied the Budget Committees to shift budget authority from defense to social programs. It achieved no particular success. "Our coalition is very skeptical about whether this process can be used to reorder priorities," said a council official.[33]

FACING THE FACTS

If the budget process did not usher in a new era of congressional budget policy, it nevertheless yielded a less tangible but highly significant benefit. It forced Congress to face the consequences of its spending and revenue decisions. No longer could Congress vote for a new program for the poor or a new tax break for business without recognizing the impact on the budget and the economy.

Sometimes the new congressional awareness made a difference. The 1976 tax bill, loaded down with tax expenditures in the Senate, might have kept many of those provisions if it had not been for Muskie's determination to oppose them on budgetary grounds. Instead, the tax bill that emerged from a House-Senate conference committee resembled the House's original version much more closely than the Senate's.

Sometimes it made no difference that Congress understood the budgetary implications of its actions. No matter how vigorously Muskie and Giaimo opposed the 1977 farm bill for busting the congressional budget, Congress approved the bill by a lopsided majority. Muskie suffered the same fate on the 1978 farm bill. But at least Muskie's and Giaimo's opponents could not help but recognize that more generous benefits for farmers meant a bigger deficit. If politics persuaded them to vote for the farmers and against sound budget policy, it was not the fault of the budget process.

On rare occasions, the Budget Committees were unable even to introduce budgetary considerations into the debate over a particular bill. The most ominous occurrence came late in 1977, when Senate Finance Committee chairman Russell Long, still smarting over his confrontation with the Budget Committee the year before, rammed an energy tax bill through the Senate floor. Long brought to the floor a bill with tax cuts that would have left total fiscal 1978 revenue below the minimum allowed in the second budget resolution for that year. To keep the bill consistent with the resolution, Long inserted a provision directing the Treasury Department to withhold the tax cuts for enough months in fiscal 1978 to prevent a breach of the revenue floor. Muskie warned that if the Budget Committee allowed that provision to remain in the bill, "then from here on we can expect similar provisions in revenue laws that would make them completely outside the budget process."[34] But Long assured the Senate that the bill that ultimately emerged from a compromise with the House would not need any such provision because it would not violate the second resolution's revenue total.[35] By swallowing Long's approach, the Senate denied itself the opportunity to examine the budgetary implications of the energy tax bill.

ADVANCE BUDGETING

Before it can get a firm grip on fiscal policy and spending priorities, Congress will have to look beyond the coming year and plan budget policy several years in advance. If Congress can do little to determine the size of the military establishment in the coming year, it can plan an increased or decreased defense manpower level for five years hence and take the first steps toward reaching that goal. It cannot appropriate less for welfare programs next year than current benefit levels require, but it can reform the welfare system in ways that could have enormous impact on benefits in years to come. Small changes in law—such as repeal of the 1-percent kicker in federal pension benefits—may not have much effect in the coming year. But the effects are compounded from year to year, and after a few years they become substantial. As the Brookings Institution found:

While the controllable portion of the budget when viewed one year at a time may look very small, over the longer run it becomes much greater.... But budgetary planning is needed to avert an overextension of commitments and to assure that the right priorities are stressed in the budget.[36]

In its 1975 study, the Brookings Institution projected the budget to fiscal 1980 and found that Congress could have considerable room to maneuver. Current federal commitments, it found, will require the expenditure of about $476 billion in 1980. But if outlays remain at the same percentage of the national economy in 1980 as they were in 1976,[37] spending will reach $501 billion. That leaves Congress about $25 billion to work with, or more if it can plan ways to reduce current commitments. The margin becomes even greater if Congress allows outlays to increase to their 1970 share of the economy. Then Congress will be able to plan for the use of about $60 billion that is not already encumbered by current commitments.[38] But as the Brookings authors pointed out, "That kind of forward planning will require a procedure in which Congress looks several years ahead, sets goals for that future date, and then works back to the present budget."[39]

The budget reform act included a number of provisions designed to force the Budget Committees and Congress to look beyond the immediate future. The Congressional Budget Office must project the five-year impact of every spending bill that goes to the House and Senate floors. At the beginning of each fiscal year, the CBO must report to Congress on spending, revenue, surplus or deficit, and tax expenditures for the coming five years. The president has to project the impact of his annual budget proposals over five years. In addition, the CBO has emphasized the five-year budget outlook in many of its budget analyses, in particular its annual report to Congress in 1977, which looked at general budget goals and eleven specific issues over the long term.[40]

The five-year planning provisions of the budget reform act were not entirely without impact on Congress. No longer could a president sell a new program to Congress, as Lyndon

Johnson sold Medicaid in 1965, by claiming its costs in the first year would be minimal and ignoring the costs in future years. Budget reform made Congress conscious of the possibility that a program that was cheap to get started could become expensive in full swing. Muskie said the budget process made him more aware of the long-term costs of national health insurance—and more reluctant to support it.[41]

But on the whole, Congress still wore blinders that blocked out everything but the coming year. The key vehicle for budget control was the budget resolution, and budget resolutions applied only to one year. Congress never had to vote on how much money it thought the government should be collecting or spending five years hence. When it adopted targets for defense spending, it did not have to ask itself how much a new weapons acquisition program would cost in five years. When it set the coming year's allowance for welfare spending, it did not have to concern itself with the long-term implications. When the Budget Committees prepared their resolutions, their staffs regularly showed them the long-range effects of various policy options. Committee members just as regularly paid little attention.

The Congressional Budget Office recommended that budget resolutions set targets not only for the coming fiscal year but for the four following years as well. Congress could and surely would amend its advance targets year by year, the CBO said, but at least it would be forced to focus on the directions in which the budget was going. "There is very little the Congress can do to make the budget of the federal government next year look much different from that of this year," the CBO found. ". . . If the goal is a balanced budget or a 4-percent unemployment rate or both or something else in 1982, it is almost a certainty we will not get there if we wait until 1981 to state the 1982 goal and do something about it. We have to begin now."[42]

The House Budget Committee leadership occasionally appealed for long-term budgeting. Adams laid before Congress in early 1976 his view of where the budget was going for the rest of the decade, but Congress—and even his own Budget Committee—virtually ignored his thoughts. If Congress could hold spending for ongoing programs below their current levels, Adams said, it would make room to reform the nation's welfare system and cut taxes in the lower brackets. But if Congress continued to look no further than the next year, it would find the budget largely outside its control. Adams said:

> We can continue to enact programs without knowing how to assess their performance, or how to evaluate the need for their continuation. We can continue to make commitments to automatic cost escalations in future years without knowing whether and how those commitments can be fulfilled. We can continue to initiate development and procurement of weapons systems without facing up to the consequences and costs of full production. In short, we can easily make poor decisions.[43]

A year later, Rep. Butler Derrick, chairman of the House Budget Committee's task force on the budget process and control, released a report on budget control that was prepared for him by Allen Schick of the Congressional Research Service. After examining a wide range of budget control issues Schick recommended, among other things, that Congress "focus more concretely and explicitly on the future consequences of current actions."[44] Derrick, hoping to draw public attention to budget control, held a press conference to release Schick's report. He found out just how interested the national press was; the only two reporters who appeared were from newspapers in Derrick's home state of South Carolina.

Congressional interest did not reach much further. Despite budget reform, Congress continued to stumble along from year to year and let a future Congress worry about the future.

CHAPTER 8

BUDGET REFORM AND THE SPENDING COMMITTEES

IF BUDGET REFORM did not revolutionize the content of spending legislation produced by Congress, it had enormous impact on the operating procedures of the committees that prepared spending bills. These committees had to work much faster than they ever had in the past. Committees responsible for legislation authorizing federal spending had to report their legislation by May 15 of each year, while those that appropriated funds faced an early September deadline for final action on their thirteen regular spending bills.

But the committees found that more than their schedules felt the impact of budget reform. For the first time, they had to fit their legislation into a congressional budget. For the most part the committees did not feel severely constrained by the budget resolutions adopted by Congress. But on occasion, the Budget Committees used budget resolutions to force revisions not only in the direct spending bills of the Appropriations Committees but also in some authorization bills.

APPROPRIATIONS COMMITTEES

Within Congress, the gravest jurisdictional threat posed by the new Budget Committees was to those congressional overlords of federal spending, the House and Senate Appropriations Committees. For more than a hundred years, the Appropriations Committees had regarded themselves as the watchdogs of the Treasury, Congress's only defense against federal spending run wild. Now the upstart Budget Committees would be deciding how much the government should spend in total each year, and what its spending priorities should be. Would the Appropriations Committees accept other committees that set outlines, however broad, for their legislation? Worse yet, would the Budget Committees encroach on the Appropriations Committees' inviolable domain —the individual line items of the budget?

The authors of the budget reform act recognized the ill will that was sure to develop in the Appropriations Commitees. To offset it, they loaded the act with provisions to pacify the two spending committees. They established a budget timetable designed to enable Congress to end one of the Appropriations Committees' great frustrations—their long-standing inability to secure the enactment of their spending bills before the beginning of the year in which they took effect. They wrote provisions to close the back doors to the Treasury—the techniques that Congress had developed to evade its frugal Appropriations Committees as it mandated federal spending. Finally, they held out the promise to the Appropriations Committees that budget reform would help them in their never-ending struggle to impose spending restraint on Congress.

But in practice, the budget reform act proved less than the Appropriations Committees had hoped. It did indeed force Congress to work faster; in 1976, for the first time in twenty-eight years, Congress finished all its regular appropriations bills before the next fiscal year began. However, the Appropriations Committees found the new deadlines too hard on them and not tough enough on the authorizing committees, which must act before appropriations can be made. To follow the new schedule, the Appropriations Committees had to sacrifice some of the thoroughness with which they had examined federal spending in the past.

Spending control proved elusive in the early years of budget reform. The Budget Committees opted for high spending targets, lest they appear to be dictating the shape of appropriations bills. The Appropriations Committees found that the targets, far from exerting any downward pressure on spending, in some cases actually encouraged Congress to spend more. Furthermore, budget reform left the back door to the Treasury partially open and unguarded by the Appropriations Committees. The provision to curb entitlements—programs that guarantee federal benefits to individuals—was too unwieldy to be effective.

But these considerations paled in comparision to that great congressional imperative—committee jurisdiction. The Appropriations Committees could tolerate budget reform as long as the Budget Committees left them free to set the size of individual federal programs. But no matter what the benefits for Congress as a whole, budget reform would be unbearable to the Appropriations Committees if they lost control of the elements of the budget. In the Senate, Muskie never missed an opportunity to remind the Appropriations Committee—and his own—that the Budget Committee was not in the business of filling in the blanks on individual budget lines. But the House Budget Committee could not resist the temptation to delve into line items, and the Appropriations Committee's concern slowly turned to anger.

Committee Relations

Richard Bolling, the primary author of budget reform in the House, realized that the new budget process would wither and die if the Appropriations Committee paid no attention to it. As he guided the budget reform act through the House, he made sure that Appropriations chairman George Mahon approved of every step. Whatever Mahon wanted,

Mahon got, including a prohibition against all backdoor spending and a March 31 deadline for enactment of authorization bills (although both provisions were watered down in compromise with the Senate). Consequently, Mahon solidly supported budget reform when it was enacted. When budget resolutions faced close votes on the House floor in 1975, the Budget Committee could count on Mahon to use his considerable prestige to plead with House members to keep the budget process alive.

The new Budget Committee took steps to keep Mahon on its side. As director of the staff experts who worked on the spending side of the budget, the Budget Committee appointed Bruce Meredith, who had served with the Appropriations Committee staff for eight years. Meredith understood the pride and the jealousy of the Appropriations Committee, and the Appropriations Committee trusted Meredith. When the Budget Committee drew up a list of ten economy measures that Congress should enact in 1976 to conform to the current budget resolution, the list looked as if it had been prepared by the Appropriations Committee. The two measures that were enacted—repeal of the 1-percent kicker for federal pension benefits and a ceiling on highway construction outlays—had long been sought by the Appropriations Committee.

But the Budget Committee was guilty of the cardinal sin— it threatened the Appropriations Committee's jurisdiction over budget line items. Budget Committee chairmen Adams and Giaimo built their budget resolution recommendations on their estimates of spending in all of the nearly eleven hundred line items of the budget. Committee members debated line items as they decided whether to modify their chairman's recommendations. So did the full House when it considered resolutions reported by the Budget Committee.

The Appropriations Committee understood that the Budget Committee could not pick the budget's functional spending totals from thin air. It knew the Budget Committee could not recommend total defense spending without judging whether the B-1 bomber should be built or set a total for veterans' benefits without considering whether GI Bill benefits should be increased. The Appropriations Committee simply wanted the Budget Committee to keep its specific recommendations out of the public record, where they might influence line items in appropriations bills. From the outset, Mahon was not satisfied that it did. When the very first budget resolution went to the House floor in 1975, he urged the Budget Committee to keep its awareness of individual spending programs out of its recommendations. "The [budget reform] act did not contemplate another voice for pet projects, and separate advice on the details of administering individual programs," he said.[1]

A year later, Mahon included his warning in the Appropriations Committee's March 15 report to the Budget Committee:

> With respect to the content of the report of the concurrent resolutions of the budget, the committee notes with concern the tendency to identify and to make recommendations for specific line items. While these line item recommendations have no actual effect, they do tend to obscure the overall macroeconomic responsibilities of the Budget Committee and to needlessly duplicate much of the hearings and deliberations that are the responsibility of the authorizing and appropriating committees.[2]

Mahon felt the Budget Committee did not get the message. After another year, the Appropriations Committee included identical language in its March 15 report. And in 1977, it added a damning indictment of the entire budget process:

> The [Appropriations] Committee is concerned about the failure of the new congressional budget process to relate the spending and revenue sides of the budget adequately. One of the principal thrusts of the budget act was to create a mechanism for the Congress to relate consciously the two sides of the budget—revenues provided by taxes and spending by various

appropriations. This has not been done, except in a generally superficial and nonanalytical manner, and certainly not in the fashion contemplated in the act.

Essentially all that has been done in the budget resolutions thus far has been to go to great lengths to detail spending policy line item by line item and only touch in the broadest way the totals of taxation policy. This approach defeats the macro-economic thrusts of the budget act and offers the potential for poor overall congressional budgetary policy.[3]

In the Senate, relations between the Appropriations and Budget Committees followed exactly the opposite course. Originally the only outspoken Senate skeptic about the budget process, Appropriations chairman John McClellan developed into a supporter as the years went by. For more than a decade before the enactment of budget reform McClellan had proposed a Joint Budget Committee to oversee federal spending and revenue policy in Congress. But his proposal never got anywhere, and when budget reform finally evolved as an initiative of other senators, McClellan did not join them. He was a member, though not an active one, of both the Joint Study Committee on Budget Control and the Senate Government Operations subcommittee that reported the first budget reform bill. When the Rules and Administration Committee mobilized staff members from the entire Senate to write the final Senate version of budget reform, the Appropriations Committee staff was conspicuous by its inactivity. McClellan found the budget reform act much too complicated to stand a good chance of success. "Possibly the greatest virtue of this particular legislation is that it may serve as a vehicle for trial and error," he said. "Experimentation with it for a year or two may demonstrate the serious flaws that it embraces and may indicate how the deficiencies and weaknesses that it contains can be eliminated."[4]

Instead of trying to appease McClellan, Muskie and his Budget Committee immediately challenged the Appropriations Committee's claim of jurisdiction over presidential impoundment proposals. McClellan was afraid that the Budget Committee would meddle in individual appropriations accounts if it had jurisdiction over impoundments, which often deal with very small pieces of the budget. After several months of deadlock, Muskie and McClellan agreed that impoundments should be referred jointly to their two committees. McClellan gained what he felt was essential—the authority to manage impoundment bills on the Senate floor.

In the first year of the new budget process, McClellan found his worst fears coming true; he was hopelessly befuddled by the first budget resolution, which was stated in terms of the sixteen budget functions, not the thirteen appropriations bills. "There is now much confusion," he said, with a touch of understatement.[5] But his bewilderment abated in 1976 as the Budget Committee, as required by the budget reform act, computed the amount of spending the budget resolution assumed under the jurisdiction of the Appropriations Committee. The Appropriations Committee, in turn, divided its spending total among its thirteen subcommittees, all of which then had a target to aim for in fiscal 1977.

McClellan was considerably relieved that Muskie, unlike the chairmen of the House Budget Committee, did not prepare budget resolutions by estimating the size of individual line items of the budget. "We do not go into the program detail that the Appropriations Committee does," Muskie said on one occasion. "If we were to do the actual allocation by appropriation bill, we would be doing the Appropriations Committee's work. That is not our responsibility."[6]

The strict timetable imposed by budget reform helped the Senate Appropriations Committee move out from under the shadow of its counterpart in the House. By tradition, appropriations bills originate in the House, and before budget reform the Senate Appropriations Committee had been willing to wait and see what the House did before preparing its spending bills. To a considerable extent, House action guided the Senate; the Senate Appropriations Committee became an appeals court for those who were dissatisfied with the funds allotted to them by the House. After 1974, the Senate committee often marked up its legislation and moved it through the Senate floor within a day or two of comparable House action. That left the Senate less time to digest what the House had done and to react to it. Thus the Senate Appropriations Committee became somewhat less dependent on the House.

In addition, the budget process strengthened McClellan's hand as he tried to consolidate his control of the thirteen Senate Appropriations subcommittees. In 1973 and 1974, McClellan had tried to establish a master plan for his committee by working with the subcommittees to set a target for each of their regular spending bills. The budget reform act, by requiring the Appropriations Committee to divide among its subcommittees the budget authority and outlays granted to it by the annual first budget resolution, added the weight of law to McClellan's effort. No longer could the thirteen subcommittees operate so independently of the chairman of the full committee.

For all these reasons, the bitterness that dominated the early relationship between the Appropriations and Budget Committees in the Senate proved temporary. As a committee studying the Senate committee system in 1976 reported:

> Relationships between the Appropriations Committee and the Budget Committee have been characterized as increasingly cooperative, based on a developing recognition that their interests are common rather than competitive.[7]

Impact on Legislation

The Appropriations Committees liked to think that the budget process had no impact on their legislation; they were not about to be bossed around by the fledgling Budget Committees. In 1975, House Budget Committee chairman Adams took the microphone on the House floor to praise the Appropriations Committee for cutting nearly as much from its defense bill as was called for in the first budget resolution for fiscal 1976. Mahon responded that the resolution "was not the controlling factor in the consideration of the items in this bill."[8] The staff of the House Appropriations Committee was particularly vehement on this score. One of them said, "I don't think the budget process has made one iota of difference."[9]

For appropriations bills in the aggregate, that's a hard statement to disprove. In the first year of budget reform, Congress cut $5.7 billion from President Ford's request for the thirteen regular appropriations bills—toward the top of the range of experience of the previous five years under President Nixon. In the second year, Congress cut $1.6 billion—still in the range of the previous five years, but toward the bottom. The $7.2 billion cut from defense in fiscal 1976 was a high for the period, but Ford submitted an unusually high request for that year. The $3.9 billion that was added to the Labor-HEW appropriations bill in fiscal 1977 also was a high, but that was a year in which Ford proposed deep cuts in domestic programs.[10] Table 4 compares fiscal 1976 and 1977 with the five previous years.

The Appropriations Committees found that budget resolutions left them more than enough room to include everything they wanted in their legislation. The Budget Committees, especially in the House, took care to use the Appropriations Committees' March 15 estimates of their spending plans as guidance in shaping their annual first budget resolutions. Even the defense totals, although less than the budget requests of the Republican president for the 1976 and 1977 fiscal years, were not far from the Appropriations Committees' estimates of what they would need. In some domestic areas, particularly energy and education, budget resolutions made room for considerably more spending than the Appropriations Committees wanted. The high targets encouraged spending proposals that many Appropriations Committee members opposed. Said one House Appropriations subcommittee staff member, "If your job is to hold down spending —the traditional Appropriations Committee view—then high targets hurt us."

For example, during eight years of Republican presidents between 1969 and 1977, Congress tried to override six vetoes of Labor-HEW appropriations bills that Presidents Nixon and Ford refused to sign because they exceeded their budget requests. Three of the vetoes preceded congressional budget reform, and Congress overrode only one. After the budget process took effect, the Budget Committees argued that the three vetoed bills were within the congressional budget, even if they exceeded the president's—and Congress overrode all three vetoes. Another example was the fiscal 1977 appropriations bill for public works, which exceeded the president's budget request by more than any other since World War II. "I attribute that in part to the new budget process," said a Senate Appropriations subcommittee staff member who worked on the bill.

The most dramatic case occurred soon after President Carter's inauguration in 1977, when the House Appropriations Committee was working on a bill appropriating funds for economic stimulus programs. Carter's stimulus recommendations, relying largely on a tax cut, included only $1.9 billion in increased outlays for the current 1977 fiscal year. But the third budget resolution for fiscal 1977, which the House Democratic leadership was instrumental in shaping, made room for $3.7 billion in new spending for job-creating programs. However, the House Appropriations Committee reported a bill that matched President Carter's policies more closely than the third budget resolution. Rep. Thomas P. O'Neill, Jr., the new House speaker, was not at all pleased, and he summoned the leaders of the Appropriations and Budget Committees to his office. Mahon explained that in his view the third resolution set a ceiling on spending, but it did not set a required spending level. Some of the items assumed

Table 4 *Congressional Impact on Appropriations Bills*
(in millions of dollars)

		1971	1972
Defense	BA	$-2,150	$-3,025
	O	-880	-1,200
Military construction	BA	-97	-93
	O	-10	-3
Foreign operations	BA	-342	-353
	O	-58	-50
Labor and Health, Education, and Welfare	BA	+240	+581
	O	+40	+225
Housing and Urban Development, independent agencies	BA	+241	+883
	O	-2	+216
Agriculture, environmental and consumer protection	BA	+343	+1,172
	O	+280	+425
State, Justice and Commerce, and the judiciary	BA	-143	-150
	O	-41	-66
Transportation	BA	-55	+45
	O	-15	+13
Public works	BA	-25	+59
	O	+16	+88
Interior	BA	-4	+29
	O	-3	+28
Treasury, Postal Service and general government	BA	-42	-280
	O	-28	-279
District of Columbia	BA	0	-17
	O	0	-17
Legislative branch	BA	-8	-6
	O	-8	-6
Total	BA	$-2,042	$-1,155
	O	-709	-626

Note: The table shows the amounts by which Congress added to or cut from the budget authority and outlay requests of Presidents Nixon and Ford for the 13 regular annual appropriations bills. For fiscal years 1971 through 1975, Congress had no

in the third resolution, Mahon said, probably were not worthwhile. O'Neill went into a rage. The budget resolution was not just a paper exercise, he said; it was a statement of the policy of the Democratic leadership. Rep. Jamie Whitten, the second-ranking Democrat on the Appropriations Committee,

1973	1974	1975	1976	1977
$-5,221	$-3,536	$-4,961	$-7,228	$-3,621
-1,750	-1.500	-2,500	-2,927	-1,370
-338	-286	-310	-524	-128
-9	-10	-23	-9	-3
-1,510	-1,212	0	-620	-684
-265	-250	-265	-190	-127
+966	+1,377	-485	+1,974	+3,943
0	+510	-425	+627	+1,731
-372	+439	-221	+565	-2,022
+34	0	-125	+2	-558
+482	+108	-59	-23	+78
+250	+250	-240	-39	+302
-23	-57	-163	+237	+367
-28	-33	-113	-2	+150
-41	-112	-239	-91	+43
-48	-30	-220	-28	+290
+16	-8	+11	+141	+305
+28	+20	+50	+120	+244
+22	+73	+15	-73	-107
+10	+75	+25	-64	-5
-9	-140	-57	-16	+308
-36	-42	-17	+12	+301
-27	-15	-27	-43	-33
-27	-14	-23	0	-28
-6	-72	-14	-11	-49
-5	-16	-11	-9	-47
$-6,016	$-3,441	$-6,510	$-5,712	$-1,600
-1,846	-1,040	-3,877	-2,507	+880

procedures with which it could relate appropriations bills to budget totals. The new congressional budget process was in effect for fiscal years 1976 and 1977.
Source: Joint Committee on Reduction of Federal Expenditures, Congressional Budget Office

said the committee was guided by Carter's recommendations. O'Neill stormed back that the budget process gave Congress a way to write the budget itself, without taking orders from the president, even if he was a Democrat. O'Neill prevailed; the Appropriations Committee rewrote its bill to correspond to the budget resolution. When he took the bill to the House floor, Mahon complained that Congress was "throwing money at our problems. . . . I would hope that we do not get stuck with too much inflation as a result of this legislation."[11]

If the budget process did not hold down spending in appropriations bills, at least it helped the Appropriations Committees close—if only part way—the various backdoor spending techniques that Congress had developed. Authorizing committees found they could no longer provide the executive branch with new authority to enter into contracts or borrow money from the Treasury unless appropriations bills permitted the spending. "I think we are making real progress," Mahon said of the prohibitions on contract and borrowing authority, "and I am highly encouraged about it."[12]

However, the Appropriations Committees were not so satisfied about the way the budget process worked with respect to another kind of backdoor spending—the entitlement. For years congressional liberals had been bypassing the spending watchdogs on the Appropriations Committees by enacting legislation that entitled individuals to federal benefits regardless of whether funds were provided in appropriations bills. The budget reform act provided that entitlement legislation, if it exceeded the most recent budget resolution's allocation of spending authority to the authorizing committee that reported the bill, must be referred to the Appropriations Committees. The Appropriations Committees would have fifteen days to attach amendments limiting the spending. In practice, this provision made a difference only with very small entitlement legislation. For example, in 1976 the House Appropriations Committee amended a spending provision out of one military pension bill and helped kill another.[13] But with larger entitlement bills, the Appropriations Committees found the budget reform act of no particular help. A member of the House Appropriations Committee staff said the committee would do just as well by trying to amend entitlement bills on the House floor.

Meeting Deadlines

Before budget reform, Congress had not enacted all its regular appropriations bills before July 1—the start of the fiscal year—since 1948. Not since 1972 had it enacted even one of the regular spending bills before July 1. Executive departments and agencies had to begin the new fiscal year spending money at the same rate as in the previous year, only to have to change course suddenly when Congress got around to determining their new appropriations. While the government was lurching into the new fiscal year, the House and Senate Appropriations Committees were taking their time. In part, their leisurely pace was forced upon them by the fact that many authorizing bills, especially those that authorized appropriations for defense and foreign aid, were not enacted until well past July 1 every year. The Appropriations Committees did not want to prepare their spending bills until they knew what programs Congress had authorized. But beyond that, the Appropriations Committees wanted to spend many months every year holding hearings to gather information to help them determine how the government should spend its money. This was especially true in the House, where Appropriations Committee members belonged to no other major committees and could concentrate on their Appropriations Committee duties.

Budget reform changed all that. In 1975, when its budget process was brand new, Congress did not try to enforce the appropriations deadlines. In 1976 it tried—and succeeded. All thirteen of its appropriations bills were in place by October 1, the new first day of the fiscal year. (Of course, the extra three months made it a lot easier for Congress to get its work done on time. But before budget reform, Congress had not enacted all its appropriations bills even by October 1 since 1961.) Executive departments and agencies knew by October 1 how much money they would be able to spend for the next twelve months. Congress was not so successful in 1977, when three of its regular appropriations bills were delayed for nearly three months beyond October 1. But the reasons had nothing to do with the budget process; for example, the bill for the Labor and HEW Departments was stalled by a disagreement over whether any of its funds should be used to pay for abortions.

For the Appropriations Committees, as for the other committees of Congress, the first requirement of the budget process was the March 15 report. The Appropriations Committees had to estimate the amount of spending they would put into their legislation—no small task, since they had jurisdiction over some 65 percent of the federal budget. In both the House and the Senate, the staffs of the Appropriations subcommittees did the bulk of the work. To prevent programs from being squeezed out of the budget, they tried to make their spending estimates err, if at all, on the high side. They based their estimates on a variety of sources: the president's budget request, their own experience, informal conversations with subcommittee members, and discussions with the staffs of the committees responsible for the legislation authorizing their appropriations. Often the staffs presented their estimates to their subcommittees at formal meetings; sometimes they simply showed their subcommittee members individually what they had prepared. The subcommittees sent their estimates on to their full committee, which incorporated them into the March 15 reports for the Budget Committees.

The March 15 reports of both Appropriations Committees used the president's budget request as their starting point. Although the congressional budget was to be a very broad statement of spending priorities, both committees were very specific in the changes they predicted Congress would make in the president's budget. For fiscal 1977, the Senate Appropriations Committee listed some tiny increases over the presidential budget: $50 million for mass transit and $10 million for veterans hospital construction.

The budget process forced many of the Appropriations subcommittees in both the House and the Senate to end their hearings weeks and even months earlier than they had in the past. The compressed hearing schedule proved especially burdensome in the House, where Appropriations Committee members devote much of their attention every year to their subcommittees. For the House subcommittees with the biggest appropriations bills, those for the Defense Department and the Labor and HEW Departments, the tight schedule was a definite hardship. In 1974, the defense subcommittee held forty-six days of hearings between February and June. In 1976, the subcommittee had time for only twenty-nine days of hearings between February and April. The subcommittee staff made many of the minor decisions itself and exposed the subcommittee members only to the major issues, such as shipbuilding for the Navy and recruiting for the volunteer Army. "As a result," said one staff aide, "subcommittee members know less about what's in the defense budget. They're no longer as effective a check and balance on executive branch spending."

Hearings were never so important to the Senate Appropriations Committee, whose members are also busy with at least one other major committee. However, the Senate committee also had to compress its hearing schedule in 1976, with one bizarre result. The Labor-HEW subcommittee, chaired by Sen. Warren G. Magnuson, was regularly unable to get a single subcommittee member to convene a hearing. The staff was unable to postpone hearings for long because of the budget reform schedule. So the staff printed the testimony of witnesses as if they actually had appeared at hearings, along with the statements prepared by staff for Magnuson and other senators. To make the hearing record realistic, the staff embellished the written statements with dialogue and even jokes. When the media revealed the phantom hearings, Harley M. Dirks, the subcommittee staff director, resigned.

Under the schedule imposed by budget reform, the thirteen House Appropriations subcommittees concluded their hearings in early April and met in late April and early May to mark up their spending bills. But at markup time, the May 15 deadline for other committees to finish work on their authorizing bills had not arrived. In many cases, the Appropriations subcommittees had to prepare legislation appropriating funds for programs whose authorizations still did not exist in the form of legislation, much less law. For example, the fiscal 1977 appropriations bill for the Energy Research and Development Administration was written before the bill to authorize appropriations was reported to the House floor. In fact, the appropriations bill was enacted and took effect months before the authorization bill was finally enacted in 1977.[14] Another good example is the 1977 defense appropriations bill, which had to be adjusted at several steps as the defense authorization bill moved through the House and Senate and finally a conference committee. "This is a serious problem in regard to the procedural mechanics of the budget act," the Appropriations Committee reported, "and threatens to undermine the whole process unless it is corrected."[15]

When the House Appropriations subcommittees prepared their spending bills in late April and early May, another crucial date in the budget process also had not arrived. Congress does not adopt budget resolutions with targets for appropriations bills until May 15, and so the Appropriations subcommittees had no budget resolution to guide them. Instead, they merely had the separate versions of the budget resolution as written by the House and Senate Budget Committees, and they could not know the resolution's ultimate shape. As a result, many of the House Appropriations subcommittees paid little attention to the budget resolution that was supposed to guide them.

Senate Appropriations subcommittees, waiting for their House counterparts to act first, marked up their bills in late May and early June—after the May 15 deadline for reporting authorizing legislation and adopting the budget resolution. Perhaps the Senate subcommittees paid more heed to the budget resolution; staff members of the defense subcommittee, whose spending targets probably were tighter than those of any other subcommittee during the early years of budget reform, said they were careful to stay within those targets. But even in the Senate the budget resolution was hardly a controlling factor.

When the budget resolution came out of conference committee shortly before May 15, the Budget Committees divided the spending total among the various congressional committees with jurisdiction over spending legislation. About 65 percent of the total went to the Appropriations Committees, which had to subdivide their allocation among their subcommittees. The Senate committee based its subcommittee allocations largely on its March 15 report to the Budget Committee. It intentionally made the budget resolution only a secondary consideration, to show that the Budget Committee was not calling the shots.[16] The House Appropriations Committee probably relied somewhat more heavily on the functional totals of the budget resolution—but not to the point where the resolution was dictating the size of its subcommittees' bills. After all, the subcommittees had prepared their legislation before there was a congressional budget resolution to guide them.

The allocation of the budget resolution's spending total among the Appropriations subcommittees helped make the resolution more meaningful to Appropriations Committee members. However, there was still room for considerable confusion and misunderstanding. The subcommittees allocations were not divided among the sixteen functions of the budget resolution; for example, the Labor-HEW subcommittees did not know how much of their allocation was for health and how much was for education. Some subcommittees, wishing to know more about what the budget resolution required of them, checked with the Budget Committees to try to find out the underlying assumptions. But the information they received was strictly unofficial; the budget reform act had not intended that budget resolutions provide such specific guidance to the Appropriations Committees.

A special provision of the budget reform act required that the House—but not the Senate—wait until its Appropriations Committee had reported all its spending bills before debating any of them on the House floor. The purpose was to force the House to look at the spending bills as a group and determine whether they reflected the spending priorities of the budget resolution. In practice, this provision had no effect at all except to delay debate on the first appropriations bill until the last one had cleared committee. Perhaps if the bills reported by the Appropriations Committee one year are in violent conflict with the budget resolution, the House will have to decide whether to modify the bills accordingly. But that time did not come in the early years of budget reform.

In the House, floor debate of the thirteen regular appropriations bills for fiscal 1977 was jammed into two weeks in June when the House had to be in session every morning and afternoon and some nights. Many authorization bills were not enacted by then, and for eight of the regular appropriations bills the Rules Committee had to waive the rule prohibiting House floor debate of appropriations bills for unauthorized programs. The Senate passed most of its appropriations bills within two weeks of House action. The appropriations bills generally sailed through the House and Senate floors and conference committee, in conformity with the budget resolution. Budget Committee chairmen regularly took the floor to thank the Appropriations Committees for keeping their legislation within the targets that the resolution had set. At no stage was a spending bill significantly changed because of the budget process.

AUTHORIZING COMMITTEES

Late in 1975, when the Budget Committees were getting ready to begin the first year with all the new budget procedures in operation, the House Budget Committee staff held a weekend retreat for other House committee staff members to explain what budget reform was going to mean to them. The Budget Committee staff outlined the whole process: the March 15 reports from the other committees, the May 15 deadline for authorizing legislation, the power of the first and second budget resolutions. When the explanation was over, a staff member of one of the authorizing committees wondered aloud, "Why do we need any other committees anymore?"

His concern was understandable. It was apparent from the outset that budget reform was going to have an enormous impact not only on the Appropriations Committees but on the authorizing committees as well. The March 15 reports would require the authorizing committees to take an early inventory of all their plans for spending legislation for the coming year. Legislation to authorize spending in subsequent appropriations bills would have to be reported by committees to the House and Senate floors by May 15—far earlier than most committees were accustomed to acting. Authorizing committees' backdoor spending bills, those that mandate spending without need of an appropriation, would be restricted; some would be expected to conform with the most recent budget resolution, while others would be out of order altogether.

If congressional committee chairmen had been fully aware of the power of the new budget process, Congress might have found budget reform much more difficult to enact. As it was, many of them began the budget reform era ignorant of the details of the new process. "Most of them weren't aware of what they voted for," said Rep. Richard Bolling, the primary author of budget reform in the House.[17] The educational process was sometimes painful. For example, House speaker Carl Albert and House Budget Committee chairman Brock Adams met with House committee chairmen early in 1975 to tell them what was expected of their upcoming March 15 report. Rep. Jack Brooks, chairman of the Government Operations Committee, admitted that he and many of his fellow chairmen were stunned by their new responsibilities. "It's

going to be a real trauma for some of these committees,"
Brooks predicted.[18]

March 15 Reports

For the authorizing committees, as for the Appropriations
Committees, March 15 was the first important date in the new
budget cycle. It was then that they had to report to the Budget
Committees on their estimates of the size of the spending
legislation that they would report to the House and Senate
floors. As Brooks had warned, March 15 was painfully early
for some committees to make even tentative decisions about
every program in their jurisdiction. Some committees—for
example, House Education and Labor and Senate Banking,
Housing and Urban Affairs—made room in their reports for
every conceivable program that the committee might authorize. A staff member of the Senate Banking Committee said
the committee did not feel it could exclude a committee member's favorite program even before hearings had been held.
"As a result," he said, "the Budget Committee had no meaningful guidance from our March 15 report."[19]

Other committees found the early deadline helpful. The
Senate Commerce Committee had prepared its tentative legislative plans early each year for several years before budget
reform began, and the March 15 report was an extension of
this effort. The March 15 report was something new to the
Senate Foreign Relations Committee, and a staff member said
the report served the useful purpose of forcing the committee
to coordinate its plans for the year.[20]

The House Budget Committee asked for March 15 reports
that included spending estimates for individual budget accounts, along with comparisons with the President's budget.
The Senate Budget Committee did not ask for as much detail,
nor did it require comparisons with the presidential budget.
By 1977, authorizing committees in both chambers, with one
exception, produced March 15 reports that the Budget Committees found satisfactory. The Senate Armed Services Com-

mittee, maintaining that it could not estimate spending before it had completed its hearings, submitted a two-page report that lacked the dollar estimates that the Budget Committee needed.

The vast majority of authorizing committees found their estimates reflected in the first budget resolutions reported by the Budget Committees. One exception was the Senate Agriculture Committee, which complained that the Senate Budget Committee assumed some unrealistic savings in agricultural programs and food stamps in the first budget resolution for fiscal 1977. "We're seeing a great facility for playing with the numbers," said a committee staff member.[21]

The May 15 Deadline

May 15 was a doubly important date in the budget process, the deadline not only for adopting the first budget resolution but also for reporting all authorizing legislation. The most consistent critic of the May 15 deadline, which sharply limited the time available to the authorizing committees to prepare their legislation, was Sen. John Stennis, chairman of the Senate Armed Services Committee. Stennis felt the authorizing committees were forced to prepare their legislation in the dark, because the final version of the annual first budget resolution was not required until the same date by which authorizing legislation had to be reported. "The schedule set forth in the congressional budget act is difficult to maintain and ought to be reviewed," the Armed Services Committee wrote.[22]

The May 15 deadline was enforced for the first time in 1976, and authorizing committees in the House had relatively little difficulty meeting it. But when committees tried to authorize programs for fiscal 1977 in legislation they reported after May 15, the Budget Committee usually forced them to delay the effective dates of their authorizations until the following year. For example, the Public Works and Transportation Committee reported a bill on September 27 to authorize construction of rivers and harbors projects in fiscal 1977.

Budget Committee chairman Adams went before the Rules
Committee to ask that the bill be forbidden to go to the House
floor with authorizations for fiscal 1977. So the Public Works
Committee agreed to insert a section into the bill making its
authorizations effective only in fiscal 1978.[23]

In the Senate, meanwhile, a few committees had to scram-
ble to meet the May 15 deadline. Overall, Senate committees
reported seventy-six bills during the three days before May
15, compared with twenty-two bills reported in those three
days the year before. The Senate Commerce Committee
alone reported twenty-three bills on May 13. Some committees reported every bill they might seek to have enacted, even
if they were not sure of the bill's value at the time. This was
reflected in some committees' batting averages. Twelve of the
sixty-four bills reported by the Senate Commerce Committee
in 1976 did not pass the Senate, compared with only five of
forty-nine the year before.

Other Senate committees had to resort to sleight of hand
to meet the May 15 deadline. They reported dummy legislation that included the amount of money to be authorized but
did not spell out in any detail how the money was to be spent.
These committees intended to hold further hearings and flesh
out their legislation with amendments to be offered on the
Senate floor—not a popular practice, because it provides
other senators with little time to study what they're voting on.
Two such bills, for clean water and solid waste disposal, were
reported by the Senate Public Works Subcommittee on Environmental Pollution—whose chairman was Muskie. The subcommittee felt the dollar totals of its two bills were all the
Budget and Appropriations Committees really needed to
keep the budget process moving. After further hearings, the
subcommittee prepared new legislation with the same spending totals for both clean water and solid waste.[24]

To give authorizing committees the flexibility to respond to
changing circumstances, the budget reform act provided that
the May 15 deadline could be waived. In the House, the Rules

Committee, with the advice of the Budget Committee, could report to the House floor a resolution waiving the May 15 deadline for authorizing legislation drawn up to meet "emergency conditions." In the Senate, the authorizing committee that sought to report legislation after May 15 was required also to report a resolution that, if the Senate adopted it, would waive the May 15 deadline. The resolution would be referred to the Budget Committee, which would be required to send it to the Senate floor, along with its recommendation, within ten days. Waivers were common and routine for many authorizing bills (many of them minor) for fiscal 1977, the first year for which the May 15 deadline was enforced. One major bill that needed a waiver was the economic stimulus bill enacted after Jimmy Carter became president in 1977. Muskie said the waiver was made necessary by "significantly changed economic circumstances."[25]

On one occasion, the Senate Budget Committee angered the Senate Interior and Insular Affairs Committee by opposing its effort to waive the May 15 deadline. The House passed a bill on May 25, 1976, to establish a Young Adult Conservation Corps to provide jobs for youths. The Senate Interior Committee, not expecting action on such legislation in 1976, had not reported any comparable bill by May 15. After the House acted, the Senate committee reported a bill on July 28, along with a resolution to waive the May 15 deadline. The Senate Budget Committee opposed a waiver, partly on grounds that no unusual circumstances had forced the Interior Committee to miss the deadline. The Budget Committee also maintained that the Young Adult Conservation Corps, at a cost of $10,000 for each new job, was too expensive and duplicated other job-creating programs. The Interior Committee argued that the Budget Committee had no business addressing the merits of the legislation. As for its failure to meet the May 15 deadline, the Interior Committee felt it should be sufficient for a committee of either the House or the Senate to report legislation. But the Budget Committee held firm, and the Senate Democratic leadership did not let the Interior Committee's request for a waiver go to the Senate floor for a vote.[26]

Backdoor Spending

Authorizing committees felt the brunt of the budget reform act's restrictions on backdoor spending. Legislation granting new contract or borrowing authority could be ruled out of order—unless it included a section providing that the new authority was effective only to the extent that funds were allocated in a subsequent appropriations bill. In the early years of budget reform, the authorizing committees did not fully understand this restriction, and a number of them prepared legislation providing new contract and borrowing authority. The House Budget Committee was especially diligent in stopping them. It kept a close watch on legislation being developed in the authorizing committees, and it notified the Appropriations Committee when it found new contract or borrowing authority. The Appropriations Committee warned the authorizing committees that it would use the budget reform act to kill the offending provisions if the authorizing committees did not kill them first. The authorizing committees, taking the threat seriously, either excised the backdoor provisions themselves or permitted floor amendments that had the same effect. In 1975, a bill extending the U.S. fishing zone to two hundred miles off shore would have given the government permanent authority to spend the license fees that it collected from fishermen. A House Appropriations subcommittee chairman offered a floor amendment, accepted by the Merchant Marine and Fisheries Committee, that subjected the spending of the fees to annual appropriations.[27] Later that year, the House Banking, Currency, and Housing Committee offered a similar amendment to a bill that would have granted the government authority to enter into certain kinds of defense contracts without subsequent appropriations legislation.[28]

A third kind of backdoor spending—the entitlement—was not made out of order by budget reform. Authorizing committees could continue to report entitlement legislation, provided that it did not exceed the spending allocated to each committee by the most recent budget resolution. Entitlement legislation in excess of the committee's allocation would be referred to the Appropriations Committee, which would have fifteen days to add an amendment limiting budget authority and outlays. In the early years of budget reform, the Appropriations Committees used this procedure to cut or kill only minor entitlements.[29]

On one occasion, the Senate Budget and Appropriations Committees had to resort to force to assure that a bill would be referred to Appropriations. The Finance Committee's version of the 1977 energy tax bill contained several entitlement programs that exceeded that committee's allocation of spending authority in the second budget resolution for fiscal 1978. The Appropriations Committee met while the energy tax bill was on the Senate floor to seek to amend the bill to kill the entitlements. On the floor, Long acceded to a motion to refer the bill to the Appropriations Committee just long enough for that committee to attach its amendment to the bill. The Appropriations Committee sent the bill back to the Senate floor in a matter of seconds. But after a brief and perfunctory debate on the merits of the entitlement programs, the Senate defeated the Appropriations Committee's amendment.[30]

Another budget reform provision relating to entitlements caused considerable annoyance among authorizing committees. The budget reform act prohibited House and Senate floor consideration of spending legislation for the coming fiscal year until Congress had adopted a budget resolution for that year. This provision was based on a logical principle: Congress should proceed with spending legislation only when it could determine whether the legislation was consistent with the congressional budget. It meant that appropriations bills could not go to the House or Senate floor until about May 15. But it also applied to entitlement legislation, which is spending legislation because it provides for spending without subsequent congressional action.

Early in 1976, Rep. James C. Corman, chairman of the House Ways and Means Subcommittee on Unemployment Compensation, tried to get Congress to enact a bill to extend federal unemployment benefits.[31] He went before the Budget Committee to request a waiver from the requirement that the legislation wait for the first budget resolution for fiscal 1977. State unemployment trust funds were going bankrupt, he argued, and they needed federal help immediately. But the Budget Committee held that the emergency was not so great that it should interfere with the principle that all spending should follow the adoption of a congressional budget. When the Budget Committee opposed the waiver, the Rules Committee declined to send Corman's bill to the House floor until May 15 had passed, and it was approved by the House only on July 20.[32]

Corman was furious. He found the budget process to be little more than another obstacle to the enactment of important social legislation. He did not blame Budget Committee chairman Adams so much as his staff:

> I think the Budget Committee staff was trying to tell the Ways and Means Committee that it doesn't have much power any more. The whole game up here is power, and the staff of the Budget Committee would like to see the committee have a veto over all the other congressional committees.[33]

Impact on Legislation

The authorizing committee legislation that felt the impact of the budget process most directly was backdoor spending legislation. While the budget process nearly eliminated new backdoor spending, it did not prohibit legislation renewing old backdoor spending programs. Congressional budget resolutions applied to such legislation exactly as it applied to appropriations bills. One example stands out: the House and Senate Agriculture Committees' 1977 farm bill. The bill, which renewed and increased federal payments to farmers, was the target of House and Senate Budget Committee opposition because it pushed agricultural spending above the target in the first budget resolution for fiscal 1978. Congress enacted the farm bill over the Budget Committees' strenuous opposition, but the Budget Committees at least succeeded in forcing Congress to recognize that it was busting its own agricultural budget.

Legislation that merely authorized spending in subsequent appropriations bills was not subject to the same budgetary controls as direct spending bills—appropriations bills and backdoor spending bills. Authorizing legislation itself could not violate a congressional budget resolution, because Congress still had an opportunity to enact an appropriations bill that would be in line with the resolution. However, the Budget Committees, especially the Senate's, sometimes tried to force authorizing legislation to be consistent with the most recent budget resolution. The Senate Budget Committee trimmed the 1975 military procurement bill, on the grounds that Congress traditionally appropriated nearly all the funds authorized for the Defense Department.

Otherwise, the authorizing committees heard from the Budget Committees only when the budget resolution included an assumption that Congress would enact particular economy legislation in the jurisdiction of an authorizing committee. This circumstance arose more frequently in the House than in the Senate, for two reasons. The House Budget Committee was much more specific than the Senate about the legislative assumptions behind the budget resolutions. And the House Appropriations Committee, whose support the Budget Committee wanted desperately to keep, urged it to pursue a number of economy measures.

Some authorizing committees resented the Budget Committees' initiatives as intrusions. Rep. James Howard, chairman of the House subcommittee with jurisdiction over the Highway Trust Fund, grew bitter when the Budget Committee worked for an outlay ceiling for highway construction even after the full House voted once against a ceiling. When Adams and Delbert Latta, the Budget Committee's Republican leader, urged the conference committee on the fiscal 1977 transportation appropriations bill to accept the ceiling in the Senate version of the bill, Howard said:

> The Committee on the Budget, through its chairman and ranking minority member, has taken it upon itself to advise the House conferees to run up the white flag and surrender—or perhaps betray might be a more appropriate word—the expressed will of the House. In all my years in the House of Representatives, I cannot recall a more arrogant reach for power than this attempt to sell out our own conference stand and reverse the majority decision of the House.[34]

Budget Committees in both the House and the Senate worked for repeal of the 1-percent kicker that retired federal workers enjoyed in their pension benefits. Their success drew mixed reviews from the Post Office and Civil Service Committees, the authorizing committees with jurisdiction over federal pensions. In the Senate, committee chairman Gale W. McGee was in Wyoming, in the middle of an unsuccessful reelection campaign, during the battle over the kicker. Sen. Ted Stevens, the ranking Republican on the subcommittee that handled civil service pensions, showed his bitterness toward the Senate Budget Committee. "I thought we still had jurisdiction," he fumed. "We have the Budget Committee writing legislation for the Committee on Post Office and Civil Service.[35]

But in the House, the response was altogether different. Rep. David Henderson, chairman of the Post Office and Civil Service Committee, was part of the committee minority that supported repeal of the 1-percent kicker, and he welcomed the Budget Committee as an ally. Even committee vice chairman Morris K. Udall, who consistently opposed repeal, had nothing but praise. He said the Budget Committee served an invaluable function as a counterweight to the special interest groups that sought more benefits from his committee. Of the budget process, Udall said, "I'm a thorough fan of this whole concept."[36]

CHAPTER 9

IMPOUNDMENT CONTROL

THE MOST CLEARLY defined purpose of budget reform was to allow Congress to control presidential impoundments. For all their complexities and ambiguities, the impoundment control provisions of the 1974 budget reform act gave Congress a workable mechanism for preventing the president from using impoundments to replace congressional policy with his own. President Nixon, whose frequent resort to impoundments had goaded Congress into enacting budget reform, resigned from office before Congress had a chance to put its impoundment control procedures into effect. Gerald Ford, his successor, at first disputed Congress's authority to stop his impoundments, but gradually he went along with the new procedures.

When Jimmy Carter became president in 1977, the Democrats controlled the White House as well as Congress, and the impoundment control procedures were no longer needed so frequently to settle policy disputes between the executive and legislative branches. But impoundment control did not become a useless anachronism. Instead, the procedures turned out to provide a policy-making tool that the president and Congress could use together. Just as supplemental appropriations had met circumstances that could not be predicted when regular spending legislation was enacted, Carter and Congress could use impoundments to stop expenditures that had been enacted into law but no longer were needed. Such action no longer had to be the president's own. Now Congress could be a full partner in the policy-making process.

170 YEARS OF IMPOUNDMENTS

After the Louisiana Purchase in 1803, the Navy no longer needed gunboats on the Mississippi River to protect the growing nation's boundaries. So, in the first recorded presidential impoundment, Thomas Jefferson refused to spend $50,000 that Congress had appropriated for that purpose. No one complained about this eminently reasonable use of the presidential management function.[1]

Thereafter, presidents withheld money for a variety of reasons—because programs could be carried out for less money than Congress provided, because wars required diversion of funds from domestic programs to defense, because presidents wanted to put the brakes on inflation. In some cases, Congress actually legislated impoundments in the form of requirements that presidents cut spending by withholding funds from programs of their choice. "Congress has demonstrated on many occasions its inability to cut expenditures when needed," wrote Louis Fisher. "Though legislators could reach agreement on the need for retrenchment, they were frequently unable, or unwilling, to make specific reductions and offend the affected constituents and interest groups."[2]

Before World War II, impoundments almost always represented funds that presidents were able to withhold because they could carry out programs according to congressional intent without spending the full amounts that Congress had made available. The 1905 and 1906 Antideficiency Acts[3] allowed the president to accelerate or decelerate spending in the event of unforeseen circumstances. In 1921 the new Bureau of the Budget determined that program managers should treat appropriations as ceilings and spend less if they could still provide all the services that Congress intended.[4] Congress endorsed this management approach, most notably in the omnibus appropriations act for fiscal 1951.[5]

Franklin Roosevelt began impounding funds for the purpose of influencing policy in 1941. Prodded by the president, Congress included in its appropriations bill for rivers and harbors that year a provision permitting the president to defer flood control projects in the interest of saving money for World War II. By the end of 1943, Roosevelt had impounded half a billion dollars in public works funds.[6] Continuing in the Roosevelt tradition, Harry Truman withheld $735 million in spending for the Air Force in 1949, after World War II was over.[7] A year later, after the Korean War had begun, he impounded $573 million in nonmilitary spending.[8] During the Vietnam War in 1966, Lyndon Johnson announced a $5.3 billion reduction in programs that he regarded as inflationary. Among the programs that suffered the deepest cuts were highway construction, housing, and education. But no programs were abolished, and about half of the savings were deferrals rather than cancellations of spending. When Congress protested, Johnson released much of the impounded money.[9] But then from 1967 to 1970, Congress enacted spending ceilings that required first Johnson and then Nixon to withhold funds from programs of their choice.[10]

After 1970, Nixon's impoundments took on a wholly new character. Sometimes the president used impoundments to save money when circumstances no longer required its expenditure, but more often he simply refused to spend the funds that Congress had provided for programs that he did not like. During his campaign for reelection in 1972 Nixon repeatedly condemned the Democratic Congress for failing to bring federal spending under control. After his reelection he put a large number of federal programs under the guillotine. Among the victims: half of the $18 billion program for sewer construction; four of the biggest federal housing programs;

seven community development programs, including urban renewal and model cities; five Agriculture Department programs; and a variety of education and health programs.

Altogether, the Nixon Administration withheld at one time as much as $18 billion in funds voted by Congress for specific purposes.[11] Fisher had this to say about the Nixon technique:

> Used with restraint and circumspection, impoundment had been used for decades without precipitating a major crisis. But during the Nixon years restraint was replaced by abandon, precedent stretched past the breaking point, and statutory authority pushed beyond legislative intent.[12]

Congress could complain, but that was about all. As long as Nixon, unlike Johnson before him, refused to bend, Congress had no procedures for prying money loose from the recalcitrant president.

Beneficiaries of programs that Nixon had terminated turned instead to federal courts. The administration tested a variety of defenses. When appropriations for particular programs did not say in so many words that the appropriated funds *must* be spent, the administration claimed discretion to spend as it saw fit. It maintained that the public debt ceiling enacted by Congress[13] gave it the authority to hold down expenditures to stay within the debt ceiling. It cited the Antideficiency Act, which had been amended in 1950 to allow that "reserves may be established to provide for contingencies, or to effect savings whenever savings are made possible by or through changes in requirements, greater efficiency of operations, or other developments subsequent to the date on which such appropriation was made available."[14] Finally, the administration fell back on a broad interpretation of the Constitution's delegation of executive power—"The executive power shall be vested in a President of the United States of America."[15]

But in nearly every case, federal judges ruled that the Nixon administration had to release the impounded funds.[16] Before enactment of budget reform in 1974, the Supreme Court did not get involved, except to turn down a request by the state of Georgia and the Nixon administration to assume original jurisdiction in a case in which Georgia sought to halt impoundments of highway, sewer, and education funds.[17] In 1975, after budget reform was in place, the Supreme Court heard an appeal of a lower court's ruling in a sewer construction case and, upholding the decision of the U.S. Court of Appeals for the District of Columbia, held that the impoundment was illegal.[18]

TITLE X

Congress was not content to let impoundments be overturned one at a time in time-consuming court actions. Both the House and the Senate passed impoundment control bills in 1973, but the bills were quite different. The Senate bill would have required impoundments to cease sixty days after they began unless the two chambers of Congress adopted resolutions allowing them to continue. The House version would have allowed impoundments to stand unless either the House or the Senate passed resolutions striking them down.[19] Unable to reconcile the two approaches, the House and the Senate attached impoundment control provisions to their budget reform bills, which had been inspired by Nixon's charge that Congress had no procedures for dealing with the overall budget in a coherent way. The strategy was sound. Impoundment control legislation, by itself, left Congress open to criticism that it was limiting presidential authority to cut spending without doing anything to provide itself with procedures to deal with the budget. Nixon probably would have vetoed an impoundment control bill, but he could hardly veto a bill designed to improve congressional budgeting.

Impoundment control became Title X of the budget reform act. Written by the staff members who put together the final version of budget reform, Title X was a novel combination of the House and Senate versions of the impoundment control bills. It divided all impoundments into two parts:

Rescissions. The president can ask Congress to rescind budget authority permanently from the budget. A rescission becomes effective only if Congress passes legislation upholding it. If Congress does not, the president must spend the money after forty-five days of continuous congressional session.

Deferrals. Without prior congressional approval, the president may defer budget authority for all or part of a fiscal year. Either the House or the Senate may force the president to spend the money immediately by passing a resolution to that effect. If the president wants to defer spending for more than a single fiscal year, he must file a new report at the beginning of each new year.[20]

The Impoundment Control Act, as Title X was called, was distinguished by an unusual amount of fuzzy language. Considerable ambiguity was necessary to make Title X satisfactory to both the House and the Senate, whose separate versions of impoundment legislation were so different. But one feature of the new law was clear: the General Accounting Office, a staff support agency of Congress, had the authority to make sure the executive branch carried out its provisions. If GAO found that the president had failed to report a rescission or a deferral, it could make the report itself. If it found that the president had incorrectly reported a rescission as a deferral, it could reclassify the impoundment as a rescission. If it found that the executive branch had refused to spend money even after Congress disallowed an impoundment, it could go to court to force the money to be spent.

So when the House and the Senate began arguing over the meaning of the Impoundment Control Act, it was GAO's job to settle the disputes. Its first ruling had an ironic result: the new act, which was designed to control impoundments, actually gave the president new authority to withhold funds voted by Congress. It was the position of Senate Budget Committee chairman Muskie that the president could impound money by means of a deferral only if the impoundment was of the routine variety authorized by the Antideficiency Act. All other impoundments—those whose purpose was to substitute presidential policy for congressional—had to be the subjects of rescission proposals. Thus, Muskie argued, the president would need legislative approval for every policy impoundment. Ullman, the first House Budget Committee chairman, felt the difference between rescissions and deferrals was strictly one of timing. A deferral, he maintained, was simply a temporary impoundment, regardless of its policy implications.

Comptroller General Elmer B. Staats, the head of GAO, decided in favor of the House interpertation. He admitted that "the act contains complex and difficult provisions, on whose interpretation reasonable men may differ." But he found that the language and legislative history of the Impoundment Control Act left "a clear impression" that the difference between a rescission and a deferral was the difference between a permanent impoundment and a temporary one. This meant that the act gave the president new authority to impound funds temporarily.[21]

IMPOUNDMENTS ON THE WANE

President Nixon never had a chance to operate under the new impoundment procedures—he resigned from office within a month of signing the budget reform act. But President Ford picked up where his predecessor had left off. For fiscal 1975 he reported what may have been a record impoundment total—$28.9 billion, comprising $4.3 billion in rescissions and $24.6 billion in deferrals. Two items accounted for the bulk of the money—$10.7 billion for highway construction and $9 billion for sewer construction.

As a rule, Congress let stand those impoundments that represented savings due to efficient program management or changing circumstances. In the first year of impoundment control, Congress passed a rescission bill allowing Ford to cut $14.5 million from an old college housing program, because a similar program recently had gone into operation.[22] And it allowed Ford to defer $301.3 million in aid for hospital construction through fiscal 1975, while Congress decided whether to maintain the program.[23]

On the other hand, Congress did not allow the president to continue using impoundments to substitute his own policies for those of Congress. It refused to rescind $102.5 million from education for the handicapped because Ford's proposal would have cut federal grants to states for this purpose in half.[24] And it overturned Ford's deferral of $50 million—half of the available funds—for planning grants for urban and rural community development.[25] As Allen Schick found:

> Congress appears to have drawn a fairly clear distinction between routine and policy impoundments. . . . The President was repeatedly rebuffed in his efforts to convert impoundment controls into reordering the budget priorities established by Congress.[26]

Policy impoundments tended to come in the form of rescission proposals, while many deferrals were routine matters of financial management. Thus Congress allowed most deferrals to stand, while it usually did not approve rescissions proposed by the president. Table 5 shows the record that President Ford compiled on impoundments.

The number and amount of proposed rescissions fell considerably between fiscal 1975 and fiscal 1977. The drop reflected the more conciliatory approach toward Congress that Ford adopted when he ran for election in 1976. When Congress passed its domestic appropriations bills for fiscal 1975 and 1976, Ford regularly proposed rescissions of the amounts that Congress added to the president's budget requests for individual programs. This strategy proved particularly annoy-

Table 5 *Congressional Action on Rescissions and Deferrals*
(in millions of dollars)

	Fiscal 1975		Fiscal 1976		Transition Quarter		Fiscal 1977		Total	
	Number	Amount	Number	Amount	Number	Amount	Number	Amount	Number	Amount
Rescissions:										
Proposed	91	$ 4,292	44	$3,329	6	$253	12	$1,075	153	$ 8,949
Approved	39	391	7	138	0	0	6	712	52	1,241
Rejected	52	3,901	37	3,191	6	253	6	363	101	7,708
Deferrals:										
Reported	159	24,574	111	8,775	6	339	52	7,048	328	40,736
Sustained	143	15,256	88	8,397	4	334	49	7,022	284	31,009
Overturned	16	9,318	23	378	2	5	3	26	44	9,727

Source: Office of Management and Budget

ing on Capitol Hill. House Appropriations Committee chairman Mahon complained, "I do not subscribe to the theory that everything the executive does is correct and right and defensible, and that everything the Congress does by way of providing additional sums or modifying sums is all wrong."[27] For fiscal 1977, Ford decided not to propose rescissions of the amounts by which Congress increased his budget requests.

The frequency of deferrals also fell after the first year of impoundment control. The figures for the first year were swelled by the giant deferrals of highway and sewer construction funds totaling nearly $20 billion. Congress overturned $9.1 billion of the highway construction deferral,[28] and the Administration released the sewer construction funds on its own. Thus the amount of funds deferred after the first year was substantially smaller.

CONTINUING DISPUTES

In the first year of impoundment control, Congress and the president fell into a series of disputes over the new procedures. The first had to do with the difference between a rescission and a deferral—the same issue that had divided the House and Senate Budget Committees. GAO may not have defined a rescission as broadly as the Senate Budget Committee had hoped, but its definition was broader than Ford's. In fiscal 1975, GAO reclassified seven of Ford's deferrals as rescissions on grounds that authority to spend the deferred funds would expire so soon after the deferral ended that there would be insufficient time to spend them. The classic case— one that produced a showdown in court between Congress and the president—involved $264 million that Congress had set aside to help low-income families own homes.

On August 22, 1974, Ford signed the Housing and Community Development Act,[29] which overhauled federal housing aid. Among its provisions was a one-year authorization to spend $264 million in previously unused funds in the homeownership program.[30] That program had already been the subject of a Nixon administration impoundment dating back to January 1973.[31] On October 4, 1974, Ford notified Congress that he was deferring the $264 million for the rest of the 1975 fiscal year, which would end on June 30, 1975.[32] That would leave only fifty-two days—until August 22—to enter into $264 million worth of housing contracts. Maintaining that fifty-two days was insufficient time, GAO reclassified the deferral as a rescission on November 6.[33]

On February 28, 1975, Congress had been in session for forty-five continuous days since GAO's rescission report. It had not passed a bill rescinding the $264 million, and so the new impoundment procedures dictated that the administration spend the money. But it did not; it acted as if the funds were still the subject of a deferral that Congress had not overturned. So on March 13, the Senate passed a resolution[34] disapproving the deferral. Still the administration refused to spend the funds. So GAO filed suit in U.S. District Court for the District of Columbia.[35] The Justice Department, defending the impoundment, maintained that the new Impoundment Control Act did not apply to an impoundment that originated before it was enacted. Furthermore, the Justice Department argued that GAO, as an agency of the legislative branch, had no right to sue the executive branch. Judge June L. Green dismissed this defense on August 20 and ordered that the $264 million be classified as a federal obligation that could result in outlays after the one-year authorization expired on August 22. But before she had a chance to rule on the merits of the case, the Department of Housing and Urban Development reinstituted the homeownership assistance program in October.

Other disputes stemmed from late impoundment reports by the president. Under the 1905 Antideficiency Act,[36] the president has thirty days from the enactment of spending legislation to apportion the funds to the agency that will be responsible for spending them. The Office of Management and Budget, acting in behalf of the president, sometimes waited until more than thirty days had elapsed before reporting impoundments. At least twice, late reports left Congress unable to force the president to spend funds proposed for rescission. In a supplemental appropriations bill[37] enacted on June 12, 1975, Congress provided $10 million that the Community Services Administration, the federal antipoverty agency, was to spend by September 30. Ford waited until July 25 to propose a rescission of the $10 million.[38] Because of two recesses, there were not forty-five days of continuous congressional session remaining before Sept. 30, and the administration did not spend the $10 million.

In a similar case more than a year later, Ford proposed the rescission on September 7, 1976, of $126.7 million appropriated for international military assistance.[39] GAO reported to Congress on September 24 that the withholding had actually begun on July 30. Because of the late report, Congress no longer had forty-five days of continuous session before it adjourned for the year. But the appropriation lapsed on September 30, and once again, Congress never had a chance to force the president to spend the money.

On one occasion, GAO found out about a late impoundment report even before the administration delivered the report to Congress. On June 27, 1975, Congress enacted a continuing resolution[40] that appropriated, among other things, an additional $10 million for summer jobs in the Youth Conservation Corps. Even though the summer had already begun, OMB did not make the funds available immediately. A number of senators and representatives notified GAO that there was no new money available in their districts. GAO investigated and reported to Congress on July 9 that OMB planned to report a deferral of the $10 million. The next day, the Senate passed a resolution[41] ordering the release of the deferred funds.

To Congress, the single most annoying feature of impoundment control was the provision that the president did not have to spend the funds proposed for rescission until forty-five days of continuous congressional session had elapsed. When authority to spend the funds expired before the time ran out—as in the cases of the $10 million for the Community Services Administration and the $126.7 million for international military assistance—the president did not have to spend the money at all. If forty-five working days had not elapsed between the time a rescission was proposed and the end of an annual session of Congress, the count had to begin all over again when the next session convened. For example, when Ford proposed five rescissions on October 4, 1974,[42] it was not possible for Congress to complete forty-five days of continuous session until the following February 28. Thus Ford was able to stretch the forty-five-day requirement into nearly five months, with Congress powerless in the meantime to force the president to spend the $182 million proposed for rescission.

Congress entertained a number of proposals to solve the problem. Legislation was introduced that would have required that spending proceed during the forty-five days, unless Congress enacted a rescission bill.[43] Another approach would have permitted Congress to force immediate spending by adopting a resolution disapproving of the rescission.[44] But the House and Senate Budget Committees, in whose jurisdiction such proposals lay, decided not to send legislation to the House and Senate floor. The committees were afraid that other members of Congress would take the opportunity to tinker with the entire budget reform act before it was clear how—or whether—the act should be modified.

The Budget and Appropriations Committees were convinced that the Ford administration intentionally timed its rescission proposals to take full advantage of the forty-five day provision. But their evidence was strictly circumstantial, and the OMB staff members responsible for preparing impoundment reports denied that this was the case. The reports required a mountain of supporting paperwork that took a long time to put together, especially in the first year or two when OMB was unfamiliar with the process. Impoundment reports had to be signed by the president, and OMB was reluctant to go to the president with every little impoundment; it tried to accumulate several reports before taking the president's time. One OMB staff member said impoundment reports were always submitted to Congress as early as possible. He added, "It looks like it should be simple, but it's pure hell."[45]

A POLICY-MAKING TOOL

After President Carter took office in 1977, impoundments did not die out as a source of conflict between Congress and the White House. But the conflicts centered on matters of policy, not procedure. For example, Congress refused to approve Carter's request that it rescind $462 million that it had appropriated in fiscal 1977 for construction of the B-1 bomber.

Even before Carter moved into the White House, impoundment control began evolving into more than just a tool to resolve conflicts. Ford's final package of rescissions, submitted three days before he left office, proved to be his most successful.[46] Of the nine rescissions that he proposed, the Carter administration withdrew one. Congress then enacted legislation[47] incorporating five of the rescissions, for a total of $664 million out of the $1,001 million that Ford had sought. It was the biggest rescission bill ever, larger than all previous ones combined.

It is instructive to look at the reasons for congressional support of some of Ford's last rescissions. Ford had recommended rescission of $721 million to build a giant nuclear-powered aircraft carrier and to modernize a nuclear cruiser, because his National Security Council had reported after the original appropriations were made that the Navy did not really need the two projects.[48] Congress could reduce military retirement pay by $144 million because inflation had not pushed pension benefits as high as Congress had expected when it appropriated retirement funds. Another $12 million could be cut from international peacekeeping because the United Nations had a smaller budget than expected.

In each case, the rescission was a response to a development after funds had been appropriated. For years supplemental appropriations had been enacted to meet spending needs that developed after regular appropriations had been completed. Rescissions became the mirror image of supplemental appropriations; they provided the president and Congress with a way to eliminate spending that proved unnecessary. Impoundment control, which began as a means for Congress to put a stop to runaway presidential power, provided the president and Congress, working together, with a new tool for managing the federal budget.

CHAPTER 10

THE BALANCE OF
BUDGETARY POWER

IMPOUNDMENT CONTROL WAS ONLY one manifestation of the broader purpose of budget reform: to put Congress on an equal footing with the president in the making of budget policy. Individual members of Congress had their own ideas about whether budget policy should be liberal or conservative, but they agreed that Congress should at least have an opportunity to determine the nation's fiscal policy and spending priorities. Senators and representatives, Democrats and Republicans—all shared the basic goal. "A Congress that cannot control spending cannot effectively control the executive branch either," said Sen. Sam Ervin, the Democrat who, in addition to serving as chairman of the Government Operations Committee, also chaired the special Senate committee to investigate Watergate.[1] Rep. John Anderson, who ranked third among the Republican leadership in the House, similarly hoped that budget reform would be "one of the most monumental reassertions of congressional prerogatives in this century."[2]

Two or three years is not enough time to judge whether Congress used budget reform to end presidential domination of budget policy. But the initial experience suggests that if the

189

balance of budgetary power is shifting from the White House to Capitol Hill, it is shifting very slowly indeed. Even before the 1974 budget reform act, the Democratic Congress had used its piecemeal legislative process to work changes in the budgets proposed to it by Republican presidents. After 1974, it continued to modify the president's budgets—in roughly the same patterns. True, Congress used its new budget process to accomplish specific legislative results, such as a small cut in the 1975 military procurement bill and the enactment of a bill in 1976 that slowed the growth of civil service pensions. But when measured against the enormity of the federal budget, these accomplishments appear insignificant.

THE PRESIDENT'S BUDGET

One might suppose that if the new budget process helped Congress wrest budgetary control from the president, then the president would have had greater difficulty turning his annual budget proposal into reality. Especially during a period with a Republican president and a Congress controlled by the Democrats, Congress would have used the budget process to replace presidential policies with its own. But to test this premise, one must have a fair idea of what Congress would have done with the president's budget if it had not had its new budget process. And as CBO director Alice Rivlin said, "Who knows what the Congress would have done without budget reform?"[3]

To eliminate such hypothetical considerations, one might compare the fate that befell presidential budget proposals before and after budget reform. But unfortunately, comparisons of this kind reveal much more than the effect of congressional action on the president's budget. Many other influences impinge on a president's budget after he submits it to Congress in the January or February preceding the beginning of the next fiscal year. More significant than congressional action can be a changing economy, which can play hob with a president's spending estimates for a variety of uncontrollable programs. As the economy slides into recession, spending rises automatically for such programs as welfare and unemployment compensation. Recessions were setting in at the beginning of the 1971 and 1975 fiscal years, and in those years actual spending turned out far greater than President Nixon initially recommended. (See Table 6, below.)

Likewise, a recession cuts into the national income—and the revenue from the federal income tax. Through no particular action by Congress, revenue in fiscal years 1971 and 1975 turned out well below the estimates in Nixon's budget proposals. When the economy heats up faster than the economists expect, revenue rises with it. The revenue increases in fiscal years 1973 and 1974 were the result not of tax increases but of an improving economy.

So one would like to compare the outcome of the president's budget proposals for fiscal 1976 and 1977—the first two years of the new congressional budget process—with that of earlier budget proposals in years with comparable economic conditions. However, the economy of the mid-1970s was without recent precedent. The recession that reached its peak in 1974 and early 1975 was the nation's worst since World War II. It was accompanied by inflation that reached an annual rate of 12 percent—by far the greatest in the postwar experience. As the economy began to recover from the recession in the 1976 fiscal year, the inflation rate fell—although inflation had risen during the recovery from previous recessions.

FISCAL POLICY

The budget process immediately provided the main arena for the continuing battle between the Republican president and the Democratic Congress over the nation's fiscal policy. For example, President Ford challenged Congress late in 1975 to couple a $28 billion tax cut with a spending cut of the same size in the fiscal 1977 budget. Two years earlier, Congress would have had no mechanism for dealing with tax cuts and spending cuts simultaneously. But now the Budget Committees were operating, and they resented Ford's initiative. Muskie observed that under the congressional budget schedule, which Ford seemed to have ignored, Congress would not even set a spending target for fiscal 1977 until the following May, which was seven months away, and there would be no ceiling until September. Muskie wondered how Ford could place a ceiling on a fiscal year for which the president himself had not yet submitted his budget request.[4] Adams said, "A spending ceiling will be enacted shortly before the new fiscal year begins in the fall, following a full review of the economic and programmatic needs of the nation. It will not emerge from thin air."[5] Congress was ultimately forced to enact a promise to consider a $395 billion spending ceiling after Ford vetoed an earlier version of a tax cut bill without any reference to a ceiling.[6] But the outlay ceiling that Congress adopted in the second budget resolution for fiscal 1977 was $413.1 billion.

During the Ford administration, Muskie and Adams repeatedly said that the more expansive fiscal policy embodied in the congressional budgets—as opposed to the more restrictive policy recommended by Ford—was responsible for the economic recovery of 1975 and 1976. "This resolution is also significant because it is Congress's budget and not merely the President's," Adams said of the second resolution for fiscal 1977. "It contains Congress's priorities for spending and our fiscal policy for reviving the nation's sagging economy—not the fiscal policy of the President. This means Congress has taken a long step on the road to recapturing control of the purse strings which have been handed to the President by default over a period of many years."[7]

The struggle between Congress and the president was not always partisan. Henry Bellmon, the Republican leader of the Senate Budget Committee, engaged in a running feud with

Ford. During preparation of the very first congressional budget, Bellmon accused the White House of using "phony" figures to make the congressional deficit appear bigger than the one proposed by the president. Now that Congress had the capability to generate its own budget data, Bellmon was able to charge that Ford was trying "to gain some political advantage over the Congress at a time when the Congress is laboring to establish budgetary discipline and is entitled to the full cooperation of the executive branch."[8]

When Jimmy Carter succeeded Ford, Budget Committee Democrats did not suddenly become the president's agents on Capitol Hill. The Budget Committees went to work on the economic stimulus proposals for fiscal 1977 that Carter sent to Congress soon after his inauguration—and increased them. When Carter withdrew support for a $50 tax rebate— the biggest component of his stimulus package—the Budget Committees duly removed the rebate from the fiscal 1977 congressional budget, but only after voicing their determination to maintain an active role in fiscal policy. "We like to think of ourselves as an independent budgetary force," Muskie said. "If we're just going to change our views with every breeze that blows from downtown, then we're just a carbon copy of what the administration sends up from month to month."[9]

Were the congressional declarations of independence just so much posturing? Or did budget reform actually enable Congress to manipulate fiscal policy in ways that had been impossible before? Table 6 compares actual total federal spending and revenue with the proposals of Republican presidents during the first two years of budget reform (fiscal 1976 and 1977) and the five previous years. As was discussed above, many factors other than congressional action conspire to modify presidential proposals. Given that qualification, Table 6 suggests that Congress expanded upon the fiscal policy of the president somewhat more with its budget process than without it.

Table 6 *Outcome of Presidential Fiscal Policy Proposals*
(in billions of dollars)

	Budget Authority	Outlays	Revenue	Surplus or Deficit
1971:				
Proposed	$218.0	$200.8	$202.1	$ 1.3
Actual	236.4	211.4	188.4	−23.0
Change	18.4	10.6	−13.7	−24.3
1972:				
Proposed	249.0	229.2	217.6	−11.6
Actual	248.1	231.9	208.6	−23.2
Change	−0.9	2.7	−9.0	−11.6
1973:				
Proposed	270.9	246.3	220.8	−25.5
Actual	276.7	246.5	232.2	−14.3
Change	5.8	0.2	11.4	11.2
1974:				
Proposed	288.0	268.7	256.0	−12.7
Actual	313.9	268.4	264.9	−3.5
Change	25.9	−0.3	8.9	9.2
1975:				
Proposed	322.1	304.4	295.0	−9.4
Actual	412.1	324.6	281.0	−43.6
Change	90.0	20.2	−14.0	−34.2
1976:				
Proposed	385.8	349.4	297.5	−51.9
Actual	415.3	366.5	300.0	−66.5
Change	29.5	17.1	2.5	−14.6
1977:				
Proposed	433.4	394.2	351.3	−43.0
Actual	470.2	401.9	356.9	−45.0
Change	36.8	7.7	5.6	−2.0

Note: The table shows how congressional action, changing economic conditions, and other factors influenced the outcome of presidential budget proposals from 1971-75, the five fiscal years immediately prior to congressional budget reform, and in 1976-77, the first two years of the new budget process. "Proposed" figures are those that the President submitted to Congress in his initial budget proposal of January or February before the beginning of each fiscal year. "Actual" figures are those measured by the Office of Management and Budget at the end of each fiscal year.
Source: Budgets of the United States Government, Fiscal Years 1973-78; House Budget Committee

Even before budget reform, Congress regularly enacted bigger spending bills than the Republican president had wanted. In three years out of five, it left the deficit considerably larger than the president had proposed, not because it had a particular fiscal policy in mind, but because that was where its individual spending decisions took it. When Congress was able to set fiscal policy goals with its new budget process, actual spending proved $17.1 billion greater than the president had sought in fiscal 1976 and $7.7 billion greater in fiscal 1977, partly because of congressional action and partly because of factors beyond congressional control. These increases were greater than those in most of the five years preceding fiscal 1976. But parts of the increases in 1976 and 1977 undoubtedly can be attributed to the fact that the economy, though recovering from recession, nevertheless proved weaker than the president had predicted at the time of his budget request.

The increases in the deficit—$14.6 billion in fiscal 1976 and $2 billion in fiscal 1977 over the president's recommendations—were right in the middle of the range of experience of the previous years. They suggest that budget reform did not enable the Democratic Congress to implement a more liberal fiscal policy. Indeed, Rivlin said that without the budget process, Congress might very well have put in place an even more expansive fiscal policy than it did.[10] The process focused attention on the deficit, and members of Congress found it very difficult to vote for budget resolutions with the enormous deficits of the mid-1970s. Without budget resolutions Congress might have approved, on a piecemeal basis, individual spending programs that would have forced the deficit even higher than it was in the 1976 and 1977 fiscal years.

Certainly the president's Office of Management and Budget was not demoralized by a Congress that had taken away its control of fiscal policy. Deputy OMB director Paul H. O'Neill said the nation's fiscal policy in 1976 and 1977 probably was closer to Ford's because of the new budget process than it would have been without it. O'Neill said the budget process finally gave OMB a way to show Congress the inflationary risks that accompany the enactment of individual spending programs without regard for their total effect on fiscal policy. Without budget reform, he said, Congress probably would have enacted even more ill-conceived programs aimed at combatting recession. "If power is being able to influence the outcome," O'Neill said, "the executive branch has more power now."[11]

If final budget resolutions were statements of congressional fiscal policy, they did not represent actual fiscal policy in the first two years of budget reform. In both the 1976 and 1977 fiscal years, the actual deficit proved $7.6 billion below the maximum allowed by the last budget resolution. The errors were on the spending side of the budget. Spending shortfalls —a result of excessively high estimates of program costs throughout the government—offset one-third to one-half of the outlay increases that Congress had allowed over President Ford's budget. They underlined the fact that even with budget reform, Congress was hardly in complete control of the nation's fiscal policy.

SPENDING PRIORITIES

Even if Congress did not use its new budget process to work any radical changes in fiscal policy, it might have taken advantage of its new tool to alter the sorts of programs that the president thought the budget should finance. But Congress, preoccupied by the nation's economic woes, devoted little of its budget debates to considerations of spending priorities.

Budget resolutions divided spending among the sixteen government functions, such as defense and health, and it would be useful to compare the outcome of the president's spending requests for each function before and after budget reform. Unfortunately, such a comparison is impossible;

OMB redefined the functions in fiscal 1976, just as budget reform began. The next best means of comparison are the thirteen annual appropriations bills. These bills provide only about 65 percent of total annual budget authority; the rest comes from various backdoor spending mechanisms. They include spending for some programs effectively outside of congressional control, such as food stamps. But they are more valuable as analytical tools because they exclude some of the most volatile types of uncontrollable spending, such as unemployment compensation.

Comparisons between appropriations bills enacted by Congress and requests made by the president can be found in Table 7, and the results are impressive. On the average, Congress made deeper cuts into the president's defense request when it was using its budget process than when it was not. At the same time, it added more to the biggest appropriations bill for social programs—the one for the Departments of Labor and Health, Education, and Welfare. These results suggest that the Democratic Congress was better able to put liberal spending priorities into effect with its new budget process than it had been previously.

However, these results are rather misleading. If Congress cut more from the Ford defense budgets of 1976 and 1977 than it had cut from the Nixon defense budgets of the previous five years, it was largely because Ford asked for larger increases than Nixon had. Beginning with fiscal 1977 and continuing into the next year, Congress demonstrated a growing concern that defense spending had fallen far enough as a share of total federal spending. Table 8 shows that in fiscal 1977, the drop in defense spending as a percentage of total outlays was smaller than it had been in the previous five years. Similarly, if Congress added more to Ford's spending requests for the Labor and HEW Departments than it added to Nixon's, it was largely because Ford's requests were relatively smaller than Nixon's. As Table 8 shows, the share of

Table 7 *Average Congressional Impact on*
Appropriations Bills
(in millions of dollars)

		1971–75	1976–77
Defense	BA	$–3,779	$–5,424
	O	–1,566	–2,148
Military construction	BA	–225	–326
	O	–11	–6
Foreign operations	BA	–683	–652
	O	–178	–158
Labor and Health, Education	BA	+536	+2,958
and Welfare	O	+70	+1,179
Housing and Urban Development,	BA	+194	–728
independent agencies	O	+25	–278
Agriculture, environmental and	BA	+409	+27
consumer protection	O	+193	+131
State, Justice and Commerce,	BA	–107	+302
and the judiciary	O	–56	+74
Transportation	BA	–80	–24
	O	–60	+131
Public works	BA	+11	+223
	O	+40	+182
Interior	BA	+27	–90
	O	+27	–34
Treasury, Postal Service and	BA	–106	+146
general government	O	–80	+156
District of Columbia	BA	–17	–38
	O	–16	–14
Legislative branch	BA	–21	–30
	O	–9	–28
Total	BA	–3,842	–3,656
	O	–1,620	–813

Note: The table compares the average annual amount by which Congress added to or cut from the budget authority (BA) and outlays (O) recommended by Presidents Nixon and Ford for the thirteen regular appropriations bills during the five years before congressional budget reform and the first two years of the new budget process. For the year-by-year figures, see Table 4.
Source: Joint Committee on Reduction of Federal Expenditures, Congressional Budget Office

Table 8 *Outlay Trends, 1971–77*

Percent of Total Outlays

	1971	1972	1973	1974	1975	1976	1977
National defense	36.3	33.4	30.4	29.2	26.6	24.6	23.8
Human resources	42.1	44.7	46.8	48.8	51.5	53.9	53.1
All other	21.6	21.9	22.8	22.0	21.9	21.5	23.1

Note: The table expresses outlays for national defense, human resources, and all other programs as a percent of total outlays for the five fiscal years before the beginning of the congressional budget process and the two years after the new process was in effect.
Source: Budget of the United States Government, Fiscal Year 1978

the budget devoted to human resources—of which the Labor-HEW appropriations bill provides a major component—fell in fiscal 1977 for the first time in six years.

So at this gross level, the statistics are contradictory. One can prove either that Congress became more liberal or that it became more conservative with the onset of budget reform. The only fair conclusion is that it is too early to reach any conclusions about the impact of budget reform on national spending priorities.

CHAPTER 11

CONCLUSIONS

HOUSE SPEAKER SAM RAYBURN once reportedly advised freshmen representatives to "go along to get along."[1] Two decades later, the fledgling House and Senate Budget Committees applied Rayburn's advice to themselves. Just as freshmen legislators can work their way into positions of influence if they follow their party's leadership, so too did the Budget Committees feel they had to establish themselves among the traditional power centers of Congress. Life for the Budget Committees was even less certain than that of freshmen congressmen; the same Congress that established the new Budget Committees could abolish them at any time. Survival had to be the Budget Committees' first goal.

It was a goal that led to considerable disappointment during the early years of budget reform. Conservatives found the Budget Committees unwilling to reduce federal spending and eliminate the deficit; liberals complained that the committees did not enable the Democratic Congress to revamp the spending priorities of a Republican president. But condemning budget reform for failing to accomplish these objectives is like criticizing Hamlet for not making you laugh—it wasn't necessarily supposed to in the first place.

To be sure, ideologues of all persuasions had hoped when budget reform was enacted that the new process would benefit their causes. That hope was one of the reasons for the nearly unanimous support the budget act received. But the ideologues were not the only supporters of budget reform; in fact, most of the act's architects were not ideologically motivated at all. They were what we might call proceduralists—they sought procedures that would make Congress a better policy-making body. The ideological content of the policy would depend on the will of Congress; the process simply would make it easier for Congress to put in place the policy of its choice.

More particularly, the proceduralists wanted to break Congress of its habit of enacting the budget bit by bit, without ever pausing to consider the whole. They asked Congress to step back from the detail twice a year, once before debating tax and spending legislation, once afterwards. Only then could Congress use the budget as the president had used it, to determine the nation's fiscal policy and spending priorities.

But before budget reform could accomplish these lofty goals, the Budget Committees had to keep the new process alive. Survival was hardly automatic, as the experience of the 1940s demonstrated. The 1946 version of budget reform failed because it offered an overly simplistic approach to a most complex subject. The 1974 reform, at the opposite extreme, embodied perhaps the most complicated set of procedures that Congress ever imposed upon itself; it threatened to collapse of its own weight. But the Budget Committees managed to implement the procedures without making them an unbearable burden on Congress.

The Budget Committees gave Congress a chance to grow accustomed to its new budget process gradually. They implemented only some of the new procedures in 1975, the first year of budget reform in action. Thus Congress quickly had to learn the difference between budget authority and outlays. But it did not have to meet the difficult budget deadlines until 1976, when it had a better understanding of the new process.

The Budget Committees operated under a peculiar handicap when they went to the House and Senate floors to seek majority support for a budget resolution. Most issues that confronted Congress had just two sides. A member either favored or opposed federal registration of handguns; either he wanted to build the B-1 bomber or he didn't. But on the budget, Congress faced a broad range of choices. On the spending side, the budget could range from extremely conservative (tight spending except for defense) to extremely liberal (more spending for domestic programs, less for defense). Any spending option could be coupled with higher or lower taxes. With so many possible combinations, even the most popular figured to be the first choice of only a small minority of the House and Senate. The Budget Committees' job: to find a combination that would be at least palatable to a majority.

The Senate Budget Committee, thanks to bipartisan cooperation, succeeded with the votes of senators who wanted to demonstrate their support of the budget process even when they found individual budget resolutions less than ideal. But in the House, where no bipartisan coalition formed around the budget process, the Budget Committee labored mightily to write budget resolutions that could draw majority support. Many conservatives and a few liberals registered consistent opposition; the Budget Committee was barely able to fashion a moderate-to-liberal majority.

The survival instinct greatly reduced the opportunities for the Budget Committees to influence budget policy in the short term. The committees only rarely tried to use the budget process to force Congress to do that which it would not otherwise have done. Their chairmen decided that the quickest way to kill budget reform was to push legislation through Congress over the opposition of important centers of congressional power. On a given issue, perhaps only a single committee would resist efforts by the Budget Committees to manipulate spending or tax legislation. But each antagonized committee would become a Budget Committee enemy, and enough enemies could gang up to wreck budget reform.

The Budget Committees did not play entirely passive roles. Muskie, the more active of the Budget Committee chairmen, battled the powerful Senate Armed Services Committee over military spending and the Finance Committee over tax reform. The House Budget Committee was sometimes drawn into a dispute, as when the Appropriations Committee enlisted its support for a ceiling on highway construction outlays. But to the extent that the Budget Committees tried to influence spending and tax legislation, they also endangered their own existence. They had to calculate how far they could go without putting themselves permanently out of business. In their early years, they did not go very far.

The first opportunity each year for the Budget Committees to influence the shape of the budget came with the first budget resolution. The first resolution—if Congress followed it —would provide a guide as Congress adopted all spending and tax legislation for the coming year. But the Budget Committees wrote first resolutions that were largely predictive. There were some notable exceptions: for example, the Senate Budget Committee's insistence, over the Finance Committee's objections, that the first resolution for fiscal 1977 include revenue gained through tax reform. And sometimes the mere act of prediction proved controversial, as Giaimo discovered when his House Budget Committee projected (accurately, as it turned out) that Congress would approve less defense spending for fiscal 1978 than the Armed Services Committee had sought. But predicting the outcome of a particular spending or tax issue usually meant accepting the plans of the committee with jurisdiction.

If the Budget Committees took a passive approach toward writing first budget resolutions, they enforced them with considerable vigor. Under the terms of the budget reform act, first resolutions merely set spending and revenue targets for subsequent legislation. But the Budget Committees often interpreted the targets as binding—as if spending could rise no higher nor revenue fall any lower than the targets. Muskie

fought the 1976 tax bill as if revenues could not be allowed
to come up a penny short of the level set by the first resolution
for fiscal 1977. In the following year, both Muskie and Giaimo
worked hard against a farm bill that exceeded the agricultural
spending target.

But few such opportunities arose, largely because first budget resolutions had been written to accommodate most legislation that the Budget Committees expected. To be sure,
there were other factors at work. Many congressional committees consciously tried to make their legislation conform to the
first resolution; they did not want to be accused of busting the
budget. And when the Budget Committees found that other
committees were preparing legislation out of step with the
resolution, they tried—often successfully—to persuade the
committees to change their legislation rather than take it to
the House or Senate floor and face a fight with the Budget
Committees. But for the most part, spending and tax bills
enacted during the early years of budget reform probably
would not have looked much different if budget reform never
had existed. If these bills conformed to the congressional
budget, it was because the Budget Committees had anticipated them when they wrote the budget.

When September arrived each year, most spending and
revenue legislation fit into the budgetary framework that had
been set by the first resolution. The Budget Committees were
content to write second resolutions that simply added up the
spending and revenue already adopted by Congress. In particular, they shrank back from employing what might have
been their greatest power—the power of reconciliation.[2] The
budget reform act empowered the Budget Committees to
include language in the second resolution directing other
committees to report legislation needed to make total spending and revenue consistent with the resolution. But reconciliation was unnecessary as long as the second resolution
merely accommodated prior congressional action on spending and revenue bills. Muskie once tried to use reconciliation
to reduce benefits for farmers after he had failed to hold the

1977 farm bill to the spending levels of the first resolution. But he was thwarted when the Agriculture Committee led a successful effort to amend the Budget Committtee's second resolution to make room for the farm bill.

If the Budget Committees adopted a generally passive strategy in their early years, budget reform nevertheless scored some significant achievements not directly related to its impact on particular pieces of legislation. Most important, budget reform forced Congress to confront the budgetary consequences of its own actions. When it considered politically popular new tax breaks in 1976, it could not, as before, ignore the impact they would have on total federal revenue, the deficit, and the general economy. When it boosted farm benefits in 1977, the Budget Committees forcefully reminded Congress that it was increasing an already formidable deficit and lifting agricultural spending to an all-time high. True, awareness of budgetary consequences often did not stop Congress from doing what it surely would have done anyway. But by revealing budgetary implications, the budget process added a measure of enlightenment to congressional decision-making.

At the same time, the new process helped Congress overcome its image of fiscal irresponsibility. No longer could the public charge that Congress was making a shambles of the national economy because it did not know what it was doing with the budget. It was still possible to oppose congressional policies—but at least they were policies that Congress had consciously chosen. Arthur F. Burns, the chairman of the Federal Reserve Board, had been one of the most vigorous critics of pre-1974 congressional procedures. After 1974, he continued to criticize Congress's spending policy as inflationary, but he praised the budget process for revealing the economic implications of that policy.

For the first time, the budget process enabled Congress to set fiscal policy. It provided a mechanism that Congress used to identify—if not to establish—the outlines of the federal budget. At last Congress knew how much the government would spend, what its deficit would be, and how the national economy might react. By focusing congressional attention on the enormous deficits of the middle 1970s, the budget process may have discouraged spending that might otherwise have been approved. But even if it had no such direct effect at all, the process still brought fiscal policy out of the closet and made Congress aware of the impact of the budget on the economy.

The budget process was more disappointing as a vehicle to force Congress to debate the government's spending priorities. Economic issues loomed so large in the early years of budget reform that they left little time for considerations of spending priorities. Besides, the Budget Committees feared the consequences of a full-scale congressional debate of priorities. Almost any senator or representative could find something to oppose in any set of priorities, and the Budget Committees did not want to go out of their way to generate opposition to the fragile new process. Even so, the budget process made it impossible for Congress to ignore the spending priorities that resulted from its individual decisions. Every budget resolution told Congress in the simplest of terms that spending for income security programs was far outstripping that for defense. This realization may not have affected how Congress divided federal spending, but at least Congress now had a mechanism to reorder spending priorities if it so chose.

The budget process proved to be a good teacher. Only a few years after 1974, congressional debates found senators and representatives arguing fine points of economics. CBO director Alice Rivlin said the quality of the budget debate in Congress rivaled that of a graduate seminar in economics.[3] Liberals who had been inclined to spend money to solve all problems learned from the budget process that the money was severely limited; no less a liberal than Muskie himself became an exponent of spending restraint and a gradual return to a balanced budget. At the same time, conservatives learned that deficits were inevitable when high unemployment rates depressed income tax revenue and boosted welfare spending. When budget resolutions went to the House floor in 1975 and 1976, the most conservative Republicans regularly offered amendments to balance the budget by slashing spending. But by 1977, they realized that spending cuts alone were insufficient, and they modified their amendment to include tax cuts to stimulate the economy and reduce the share of the economy controlled by the government.

The more educated Congress was also a better informed Congress. The Budget Committees' staffs—and especially the Congressional Budget Office—provided Congress with information that it had never had before. At last, Congress could compute for itself the effect of its individual spending and revenue decisions on the overall budget. No longer could it be bullied by an executive branch that, given its monopoly over budget estimates, could manipulate the figures to suit its own policies. And now Congress had the capacity to add up, day by day, the cumulative effect of its spending and revenue decisions on the total budget. Before budget reform, the overall size and shape of the budget were revealed only at the end of each fiscal year. Now Congress could tell where it was going before it got there.

The Congressional Budget Office also made available to Congress its own source of policy analysis. Congress did not have to rely any longer on the executive branch to tell it which programs could meet its goals most effectively. The CBO could report to Congress on the relative costs and benefits of different military manpower levels, of alternative energy conservation programs, and of various welfare reform schemes. Its own source of policy analysis was not a sufficient condition for congressional independence of the executive branch in the setting of budget policy. But it was a necessary condition; Congress would never be truly independent without it.

Independence from the executive branch—that was one of the goals that united the senators and representatives who wrote the budget reform act in 1974. They worked at a time of bitter confrontation between a Republican president and a Democratic Congress. But the need for an independent budget-making capacity in Congress did not disappear with the inauguration of a Democratic president in 1977. Although the congressional majority was more in tune with President Carter than it had been with Presidents Nixon and Ford, it remained determined to put its own imprint on federal policy. The budget process helped make that possible, and Congress used it to modify many of Carter's budgetary proposals. As Rivlin said, "It now looks as though the budget process is part of the accepted process of making legislation."[4]

If the budget process had not become a major factor in the shaping of legislation, the potential was there. Budget reform taught Congress to confront issues of fiscal policy and spending priorities; it remained for Congress to use the process to determine its responses. As long as budget reform survived, it held out the promise of enabling Congress to make enlightened budget policy. Perhaps, as Hamilton had expected nearly two hundred years earlier, the power over the purse would at last become "the most complete and effectual weapon with which any constitution can arm the immediate representatives of the people."

APPENDIX A

HOUSE AND SENATE BUDGET COMMITTEE MEMBERS

Budget Committee Members: House

1974

Democrats	Republicans
Al Ullman, Ore., chairman†	John J. Rhodes, Ariz.‡
Jamie L. Whitten, Miss.*	Elford A. Cederberg, Mich.*
Richard Bolling, Mo.	Joel T. Broyhill, Va.†
Thomas P. O'Neill, Jr., Mass.‡	Robert H. Michel, Ill.*
Martha W. Griffiths, Mich.†	Delbert L. Latta, Ohio
Jim Wright, Tex.	Herman T. Schneebeli, Pa.†
Thomas L. Ashley, Ohio	James T. Broyhill, N.C.
Robert N. Giaimo, Conn.*	Del Clawson, Calif.
Neal Smith, Iowa*	James F. Hastings, N.Y.
James A. Burke, Mass.†	
James G. O'Hara, Mich.	
Robert L. Leggett, Calif.	
Brock Adams, Wash.	
Parren J. Mitchell, Md.	

*Appropriations Committee representative
†Ways and Means Committee representative
‡Party leadership representative

1975

Democrats	*Republicans*
Brock Adams, Wash., chairman	Delbert L. Latta, Ohio
Thomas P. O'Neill, Jr., Mass.‡	Elford A. Cederberg, Mich.*
Jim Wright, Tex.	Herman T. Schneebeli, Pa.†
Thomas L. Ashley, Ohio	James T. Broyhill, N.C.
Robert N. Giaimo, Conn.*	Del Clawson, Calif.
Neal Smith, Iowa*	James F. Hastings, N.Y.
James G. O'Hara, Mich.	Garner E. Shriver, Kan.*
Robert L. Leggett, Calif.	Barber B. Conable, Jr., N.Y.†‡
Parren J. Mitchell, Md.	
Omar Burleson, Tex.†	
Phil M. Landrum, Ga.†	
Sam M. Gibbons, Fla.†	
Patsy T. Mink, Hawaii	
Louis Stokes, Ohio*	
Harold Runnels, N.M.	
Elizabeth Holtzman, N.Y.	
Butler Derrick, S.C.	

1976

Democrats	*Republicans*
Brock Adams, Wash., chairman	Delbert L. Latta, Ohio
Thomas P. O'Neill, Jr., Mass.‡	Elford A. Cederberg, Mich.*
Jim Wright, Tex.	Herman T. Schneebeli, Pa.†
Thomas L. Ashley, Ohio	James T. Broyhill, N.C.
Robert N. Giaimo, Conn.*	Del Clawson, Calif.
Neal Smith, Iowa*	Garner E. Shriver, Kan.*
James G. O'Hara, Mich.	Barber B. Conable, Jr., N.Y.†‡
Robert L. Leggett, Calif.	Marjorie S. Holt, Md.
Parren J. Mitchell, Md.	
Omar Burleson, Tex.†	
Phil M. Landrum, Ga.†	
Sam M. Gibbons, Fla.†	
Patsy T. Mink, Hawaii	
Louis Stokes, Ohio*	
Harold Runnels, N.M.	
Elizabeth Holtzman, N.Y.	
Butler Derrick, S.C.	

1977

Democrats	*Republicans*
Robert N. Giaimo, Conn., chairman*	Delbert L. Latta, Ohio
Jim Wright, Tex.‡	James T. Broyhill, N.C.
Thomas L. Ashley, Ohio	Barber B. Conable, Jr., N.Y.†
Robert L. Leggett, Calif.	Marjorie S. Holt, Md.
Parren J. Mitchell, Md.	John H. Rousselot, Calif.
Omar Burleson, Tex.†	John J. Duncan, Tenn.†
Louis Stokes, Ohio*	Clair W. Burgener, Calif.*
Elizabeth Holtzman, N.Y.	Ralph S. Regula, Ohio*
Butler Derrick, S.C.	
Otis G. Pike, N.Y.†	
Donald M. Fraser, Minn.	
David R. Obey, Wis.*	
William Lehman, Fla.	
Paul Simon, Ill.	
Joseph L. Fisher, Va.†	
Norman Y. Mineta, Calif.	
Jim Mattox, Tex.	

Budget Committee Members: Senate

1974

Democrats	*Republicans*
Edmund S. Muskie, Maine, chairman	Peter H. Dominick, Colo.
Warren G. Magnuson, Wash.	Milton R. Young, N.D.
Frank E. Moss, Utah	Roman L. Hruska, Neb.
Walter F. Mondale, Minn.	Jacob K. Javits, N.Y.
Ernest F. Hollings, S.C.	Paul J. Fannin, Ariz.
Alan Cranston, Calif.	Robert Dole, Kan.
Lawton Chiles, Fla.	
James Abourezk, S.D.	
Joseph R. Biden, Jr., Del.	

Budget Committee Members

1975–76

Democrats	*Republicans*
Edmund S. Muskie, Maine, chairman	Henry Bellmon, Okla.
Warren G. Magnuson, Wash.	Robert Dole, Kan.
Frank E. Moss, Utah	J. Glenn Beall, Md.
Walter F. Mondale, Minn.	James L. Buckley, N.Y.
Ernest F. Hollings, S.C.	James A. McClure, Idaho
Alan Cranston, Calif.	Pete V. Domenici, N.M.
Lawton Chiles, Fla.	
James Abourezk, S.D.	
Joseph R. Biden, Jr., Del.	
Sam Nunn, Ga.	

1977

Democrats	*Republicans*
Edmund S. Muskie, Maine, chairman	Henry Bellmon, Okla.
Warren G. Magnuson, Wash.	Robert Dole, Kan.
Ernest F. Hollings, S.C.	James A. McClure, Idaho
Alan Cranston, Calif.	Pete V. Domenici, N.M.
Lawton Chiles, Fla.	S.I. Hayakawa, Calif.
James Abourezk, S.D.	H. John Heinz III, Pa.
Joseph R. Biden, Jr., Del.	
J. Bennett Johnston, Jr., La.	
Wendell R. Anderson, Minn.	
James R. Sasser, Tenn.	

BUDGET RESOLUTIONS:

House and Senate Versions Compared with
Presidential Requests (in Billions of Dollars)
for Fiscal 1976, 1977, and 1978

Note: The tables compare congressional budget resolutions
—House-passed and Senate-passed versions as well as the
ultimately adopted versions—with presidential budget requests for the first three years of budget reform. In addition,
they record the votes by which the House and Senate adopted
the resolutions.

FISCAL 1976

	Ford Request	First Resolution (H. Con. Res. 218)			Second Resolution (H. Con. Res. 466)		
		House Version	Senate Version	Final Version	House Version	Senate Version	Final Version
Budget Authority	$385.8	$395.9	$388.6	$395.8	$408.0	$406.2	$408.0
Outlays	349.4	368.2	365.0	367.0	373.9	375.6	374.9
Revenue	297.5	298.2	297.8	298.2	301.8	300.8	300.8
Deficit	51.9	70.0	67.2	68.8	72.1	74.8	74.1
National Debt	605.9	619.9	617.6	617.6	620.5	623.2	622.6
Budget Authority:							
National defense	107.7	100.5	101.0	100.7	100.4	101.5	101.0
International affairs	12.6	4.7	6.0	4.9	6.0	6.0	6.0
General science, space and technology	4.7	4.7	4.7	4.7	4.7	4.7	4.7
Natural resources, environment, and energy	12.2	14.1	13.4	13.8	18.6	18.8	18.7
Agriculture	4.3	4.3	4.3	4.3	4.1	4.1	4.1
Commerce and transportation	6.6	11.0	9.5	11.3	17.3	19.1	19.0
Community and regional development	5.2	10.8	6.0	11.0	10.6	8.5	9.5
Education, training, employment, and social services	13.7	19.0	20.7	19.0	23.8	19.6	21.3
Health	31.0	33.1	32.6	33.1	33.6	33.5	33.6
Income security	135.3	141.3	138.5	140.9	137.6	137.3	137.5
Veterans benefits and services	16.2	18.0	17.6	18.0	19.9	19.9	19.9
Law enforcement and justice	3.2	3.3	3.3	3.3	3.3	3.3	3.3
General government	3.3	3.3	3.3	3.3	3.3	3.4	3.3
Revenue sharing and general purpose fiscal assistance	7.3	7.3	7.3	7.3	7.3	7.3	7.3
Interest	34.4	35.0	35.5	35.0	35.4	35.2	35.4
Allowances	8.3	1.7	1.3	1.4	0.8	0.6	0.5
Offsetting receipts	-20.2	-16.2	-16.2	-16.2	-18.6	-16.6	-17.1

Outlays:							
National defense	94.0	90.2	91.2	90.7	91.6	92.1	91.9
International affairs	6.3	5.0	4.9	4.9	5.0	4.8	4.9
General science, space and technology	4.6	4.6	4.6	4.6	4.6	4.6	4.6
Natural resources, environment, and energy	10.0	11.5	11.7	11.6	11.2	11.5	11.4
Agriculture	1.8	1.8	2.0	1.8	2.6	2.6	2.6
Commerce and transportation	13.7	18.5	16.6	17.5	18.6	18.3	18.3
Community and regional development	5.9	9.0	6.6	8.65	7.0	7.1	7.0
Education, training, employment, and social services	14.6	20.4	19.4	19.85	21.3	20.9	20.9
Health	28.0	30.7	31.0	30.7	32.9	33.0	32.9
Income security	118.7	124.9	126.1	125.3	128.5	128.1	128.2
Veterans benefits and services	15.6	17.5	16.9	17.5	19.1	19.1	19.1
Law enforcement and justice	3.3	3.4	3.4	3.4	3.4	3.4	3.4
General government	3.2	3.4	3.2	3.3	3.3	3.3	3.3
Revenue sharing and general purpose fiscal assistance	7.2	7.2	7.2	7.2	7.3	7.3	7.3
Interest	34.4	35.0	35.3	35.0	35.4	35.2	35.4
Allowances	8.0	1.5	1.1	1.2	0.9	0.9	0.8
Offsetting receipts	-20.2	-16.2	-16.2	-16.2	-18.6	-16.6	-17.1
Floor votes:							
House:							
Total		200-196		230-193	225-191		189-187
Democrats		197-68		225-55	214-67		186-61
Republicans		3-128		5-138	11-124		3-126
Senate:							
Total			69-22	voice		69-23	74-19
Democrats			50-4	vote		50-8	53-4
Republicans			19-18			19-15	21-15

215

FISCAL 1977

	Ford Request	First Resolution (S. Con. Res. 109)			Second Resolution (S. Con. Res. 139)		
		House Version	Senate Version	Final Version	House Version	Senate Version	Final Version
Budget Authority	$433.4	$454.1	$454.9	$454.2	$452.6	$447.5	$451.55
Outlays	394.2	415.4	412.6	413.3	413.2	412.8	413.1
Revenue	351.3	363.0	362.4	362.5	362.5	362.0	362.5
Deficit	43.0	52.4	50.2	50.8	50.7	50.8	50.6
National Debt	719.5	713.7	711.5	713.1	700.0	701.0	700.0
Budget Authority:							
National defense	114.9	112.0	113.0	112.5	112.1	112.1	112.1
International affairs	9.7	9.2	9.1	9.1	8.8	9.1	8.9
General science, space and technology	4.6	4.6	4.6	4.6	4.6	4.6	4.6
Natural resources, environment, and energy	9.7	14.8	18.0	17.0	17.9	18.2	18.2
Agriculture	2.3	2.3	2.3	2.3	2.3	1.6	2.1
Commerce and transportation	17.9	19.9	16.1	18.2	17.7	15.2	17.2
Community and regional development	5.8	6.5	7.4	7.4	9.6	7.5	9.55
Education, training, employment, and social services	15.9	24.6	22.4	24.6	23.9	24.0	24.0
Health	38.0	39.2	40.4	39.3	40.5	40.5	40.5
Income security	157.7	156.8	163.7	158.9	155.9	156.2	155.9
Veterans benefits and services	17.7	20.5	20.0	20.1	20.3	20.3	20.3
Law enforcement and justice	3.3	3.4	3.3	3.4	3.5	3.5	3.5
General government	3.5	3.5	3.7	3.6	3.6	3.6	3.6
Revenue sharing and general purpose fiscal assistance	7.3	7.3	7.3	7.35	7.6	7.6	7.6
Interest	41.3	41.4	40.4	40.4	40.4	39.6	39.6
Allowances	2.6	4.9	0.6	2.85	0.9	0.7	0.7
Offsetting receipts	-18.8	-16.9	-17.4	-17.4	-16.9	-16.8	-16.8

Outlays:							
National defense	101.1	100.6	100.9	100.8	100.6	100.7	100.65
International affairs	6.8	6.5	7.0	6.6	6.8	6.9	6.9
General science, space and technology	4.5	4.5	4.5	4.5	4.5	4.5	4.5
Natural resources, environment, and energy	13.8	15.7	15.6	15.7	16.2	16.0	16.2
Agriculture	1.7	2.0	1.9	2.0	2.2	2.0	2.2
Commerce and transportation	16.5	17.7	18.6	17.7	17.0	17.4	17.4
Community and regional development	5.5	6.2	7.8	7.8	9.1	9.0	9.05
Education, training, employment, and social services	16.6	23.0	21.2	23.0	22.2	22.3	22.2
Health	34.4	38.2	37.6	37.9	39.0	38.8	38.9
Income security	137.1	139.2	140.1	139.3	137.0	137.3	137.2
Veterans benefits and services	17.2	20.0	19.3	19.5	19.5	19.5	19.5
Law enforcement and justice	3.4	3.5	3.4	3.5	3.6	3.6	3.6
General government	3.4	3.5	3.6	3.5	3.5	3.5	3.5
Revenue sharing and general purpose fiscal assistance	7.4	7.4	7.4	7.35	7.7	7.7	7.7
Interest	41.3	41.4	40.4	40.4	40.4	39.6	39.6
Allowances	2.3	3.0	0.7	1.15	0.9	0.8	0.8
Offsetting receipts	-18.8	-16.9	-17.4	-17.4	-16.9	-16.8	-16.8
Floor votes:							
House:							
Total		221-155		224-170	227-151		234-143
Democrats		208-44		214-45	215-38		213-36
Republicans		13-111		10-125	12-113		21-107
Senate:							
Total			62-22	65-29		55-23	66-20
Democrats			45-6	49-9		41-5	51-3
Republicans			17-16	16-20		14-18	15-17

FISCAL 1977 (cont.)

	Third Resolution (S. Con. Res. 10)			Revised Third Resolution (S. Con. Res. 19)		
	House Version	Senate Version	Final Version	House Version	Senate Version	Final Version
Budget Authority	$477.9	$467.0	$472.9	$469.7	$469.8	$470.2
Outlays	419.1	415.0	417.45	414.2	408.8	409.2
Revenue	348.8	346.8	347.7	355.0	349.3	356.6
Deficit	70.3	68.2	69.75	59.2	59.5	52.6
National Debt	718.9	718.3	718.4	708.0	708.3	701.3
Budget Authority:						
National defense	108.8	109.2	108.8	108.8	108.8	108.8
International affairs	8.0	7.9	7.9	7.9	7.9	7.9
General science, space and technology	4.5	4.5	4.5	4.5	4.5	4.5
Natural resources, environment, and energy	18.6	18.8	18.7	18.7	18.7	18.7
Agriculture	2.4	1.6	2.3	2.3	2.3	2.3
Commerce and transportation	17.3	17.3	17.3	17.3	17.3	17.3
Community and regional development	15.0	14.3	14.8	14.8	14.8	14.8
Education, training, employment, and social services	30.4	30.4	30.4	30.4	30.4	30.4
Health	40.7	40.6	40.6	40.6	40.6	40.6
Income security	175.0	166.3	170.9	167.7	167.3	167.7
Veterans benefits and services	18.9	18.9	18.9	18.9	18.9	18.9
Law enforcement and justice	3.5	3.5	3.5	3.5	3.5	3.5
General government	3.6	3.5	3.5	3.5	3.5	3.5
Revenue sharing and general purpose fiscal assistance	7.6	7.6	7.6	7.6	7.6	7.6
Interest	38.3	37.9	38.0	38.0	38.0	38.0
Allowances	0.8	0.8	0.8	0.8	0.8	0.8
Offsetting receipts	-15.3	-16.1	-15.6	-15.6	-15.1	-15.1

Outlays:

	(1)	(2)	(3)	(4)	(5)	(6)
National defense	100.1	100.1	100.1	100.1	98.9	98.9
International affairs	6.8	6.8	6.8	6.8	6.5	6.5
General science, space and technology	4.4	4.4	4.4	4.4	4.6	4.6
Natural resources, environment, and energy	17.2	17.2	17.2	17.2	15.8	16.1
Agriculture	3.0	3.0	3.0	3.0	4.5	4.5
Commerce and transportation	16.0	16.0	16.0	16.0	14.9	14.9
Community and regional development	10.8	10.0	10.55	10.5	10.1	10.1
Education, training, employment, and social services	22.6	23.2	22.7	22.7	20.9	20.9
Health	39.3	39.5	39.3	39.3	39.0	39.0
Income security	142.0	139.3	141.3	138.1	136.9	137.1
Veterans benefits and services	18.1	18.1	18.1	18.1	18.1	18.1
Law enforcement and justice	3.7	3.6	3.6	3.6	3.6	3.6
General government	3.6	3.5	3.5	3.5	3.7	3.6
Revenue sharing and general purpose fiscal assistance	7.7	7.7	7.7	7.7	7.7	7.7
Interest	38.3	37.9	38.0	38.0	38.0	38.0
Allowances	0.8	0.8	0.8	0.8	0.7	0.7
Offsetting receipts	−15.3	−16.1	−15.6	−15.6	−15.1	−15.1

Floor votes:

	(1)	(2)	(3)	(4)	(5)	(6)
House:						
Total	239-169		226-173			
Democrats	225-50		218-51			
Republicans	14-119		8-122			
Senate:						
Total		72-20	voice vote			
Democrats		55-3				
Republicans		17-17				

Incorporated into first resolution for fiscal 1978. House voted down one version of the resolution, 84-320 (D 82-185, R 2-135), before Budget Committee revised it to make it acceptable.

219

FISCAL 1978

	Ford Request	Carter Request	First Resolution (S. Con. Res. 19)			Second Resolution (H. Con. Res. 341)		
			House Version	Senate Version	Final Version	House Version	Senate Version	Final Version
Budget Authority	$480.4	$507.3	$502.3	$504.6	$503.45	$508.0	$501.4	$500.1
Outlays	440.0	459.4	464.5	459.2	460.95	459.6	459.9	458.25
Revenue	393.0	401.6	398.1	395.7	396.3	397.9	394.8	397.0
Deficit	47.0	57.7	66.4	63.5	64.65	61.6	65.1	61.25
National Debt	785.0	794.7	792.7	789.9	784.9	781.9	779.3	775.45
Budget Authority:								
National defense	122.9	120.1	117.1	120.3	118.5	116.3	116.6	116.4
International affairs	9.0	10.3	9.5	9.3	9.3	7.9	8.3	8.0
General science, space and technology	4.9	4.9	4.9	4.9	4.9	4.9	4.9	4.9
Natural resources, environment, and energy	19.1	20.5	20.9	20.5	20.7	21.6	24.9	24.6
Agriculture	2.7	2.7	2.2	2.2	2.2	2.1	2.1	2.1
Commerce and transportation	18.7	19.5	20.6	19.4	20.0	22.4	20.5	20.4
Community and regional development	6.4	9.4	8.2	8.1	8.2	8.1	8.2	8.2
Education, training, employment, and social services	18.0	26.7	22.7	27.1	26.8	26.7	26.1	26.3
Health	47.4	47.8	47.7	48.0	47.9	47.7	47.7	47.7
Income security	170.2	179.8	182.7	179.9	179.9	186.8	178.8	178.6
Veterans benefits and services	18.2	19.1	20.2	20.3	20.25	20.4	19.9	19.9
Law enforcement and justice	3.7	3.8	3.6	3.8	3.7	3.8	3.8	3.8
General government	3.9	3.8	3.9	3.8	3.8	3.8	3.8	3.8
Revenue sharing and general purpose fiscal assistance	9.1	10.7	9.8	9.8	9.8	9.6	9.6	9.6
Interest	39.7	41.8	43.0	43.0	43.0	41.7	41.7	41.7
Allowances	2.9	2.9	1.1	0.8	0.8	1.0	0.9	0.9
Offsetting receipts	-16.4	-16.7	-16.0	-16.6	-16.3	-16.8	-16.4	-16.8

Outlays:								
National defense	112.3	111.9	109.9	111.6	111.0	110.3	110.1	110.1
International affairs	7.3	7.8	7.4	7.3	7.3	6.6	6.6	6.6
General science, space and technology	4.7	4.7	4.7	4.7	4.7	4.7	4.7	4.7
Natural resources, environment, and energy	19.7	20.5	20.7	19.9	20.0	19.7	20.8	20.0
Agriculture	2.3	2.3	4.4	3.7	4.35	6.3	6.3	6.3
Commerce and transportation	19.3	20.1	20.3	19.1	19.4	19.7	19.6	19.6
Community and regional development	7.9	10.1	10.9	10.7	10.8	10.4	10.6	10.6
Education, training, employment, and social services	19.4	26.5	27.8	27.0	27.2	26.9	26.4	26.4
Health	43.2	44.5	44.2	44.4	44.3	44.2	44.2	44.2
Income security	143.9	146.5	148.3	145.9	146.7	146.9	146.6	146.1
Veterans benefits and services	18.3	19.1	20.2	20.2	20.2	20.4	20.2	20.2
Law enforcement and justice	3.9	3.9	3.8	3.9	3.85	4.0	4.0	4.0
General government	3.9	3.8	4.0	3.8	3.85	3.8	3.8	3.85
Revenue sharing and general purpose fiscal assistance	8.1	9.7	9.8	9.7	9.7	9.7	9.7	9.7
Interest	39.7	41.8	43.0	43.0	43.0	41.7	41.7	41.7
Allowances	2.7	2.7	1.0	0.9	0.9	1.1	1.0	1.0
Offsetting receipts	-16.4	-16.7	-16.0	-16.6	-16.3	-16.8	-16.4	-16.8
Floor votes:								
House:								
Total			213-179		221-177	199-188		215-187
Democrats			206-58		192-70	195-59		211-55
Republicans			7-121		29-107	4-129		4-132
Senate:								
Total				56-31	54-23		63-21	68-21
Democrats				41-14	37-11		47-8	49-8
Republicans				15-17	17-12		17-13	19-13

221

NOTES

CHAPTER 1

1. United States Constitution, Article I, Section 8.
2. *The Federalist,* No. 58.
3. U.S., Congress, Senate, *Congressional Record,* 93d Cong., 2d sess. (March 19, 1974): S 3832.
4. The old Bureau of the Budget was reorganized into the Office of Management and Budget in 1970.
5. *Cong. Rec.* (March 19, 1974): S 3839.
6. U.S., Congress, House of Representatives, *Congressional Globe,* 38th Cong., 2d sess. (March 2, 1865): 1312.
7. Ibid.: 1316.
8. *Cong. Rec.* (December 9, 1885): 148.
9. Ibid. (December 14, 1885): 171.
10. Louis Fisher, *Presidential Spending Power* (Princeton: Princeton University Press, 1975), pp. 19–24.
11. *Cong. Rec.* (June 1, 1920): 8103.
12. Ibid. (June 6, 1946): 6368.
13. Low economic growth and high unemployment rates automatically reduced income tax revenues and increased spending for welfare and unemployment programs. In the mid-1970s, it was estimated that every increase of one percentage point in the unemployment rate added $16 billion to the federal deficit.
14. Arthur M. Schlesinger, Jr., *The Imperial Presidency* (Boston: Houghton Mifflin Co., 1973), pp. 252–53.
15. See Arthur M. Schlesinger, Sr., "Our Presidents: A Rating by 75 Historians," *The New York Times Magazine* (July 29, 1962): pp. 12, 40–43.
16. Clinton Rossiter, *The American Presidency* (New York: Harcourt, Brace and Co., 1956), p. 138.
17. Thomas E. Cronin, "The Textbook Presidency and Political Science," paper delivered to the American Political Science Association in September 1970 and reprinted in *Cong. Rec.* (Oct. 5, 1970): S 17102–17115.

18. Schlesinger, Jr., *The Imperial Presidency,* p. 124.

19. Harris Survey, January, 1974.

20. The Technology Assessment Act of 1972 (86 Stat 797).

21. Clark F. Norton, *Congressional Review, Deferral and Disapproval of Executive Actions: A Summary and an Inventory of Statutory Authority* (Washington: Congressional Research Service, April 30, 1976), p. 8.

22. Gerald R. Ford, *The War Powers Resolution* (Washington: American Enterprise Institute Reprint No. 69, June, 1977), p. 4.

23. Roger H. Davidson and Walter J. Oleszek, *Congress Against Itself* (Bloomington: Indiana University Press, 1977), p. 37.

24. See Davidson and Oleszek, *Congress Against Itself,* pp. 43–49.

25. Nelson W. Polsby, *Congress and the Presidency* (Englewood Cliffs, N.J.: Prentice-Hall, Inc., 1971), p. 65.

26. See Michael J. Malbin, "House Democrats Are Playing with a Strong Leadership Lineup," *National Journal,* vol. 9, no. 25 (June 18, 1977): p. 944, for an example of Rayburn's technique.

27. Richard E. Cohen, "Marking an End to the Senate's Mansfield Era," *National Journal,* vol. 8, no. 51–52 (December 25, 1976): p. 1803.

28. Remarks during a House–Senate conference committee meeting on budget reform legislation, June 5, 1974.

CHAPTER 2

1. *Cong. Rec.* (February 20, 1947): 1207.

2. Ibid. (February 26, 1947): 1438.

3. Ibid. (February 27, 1948): 1878.

4. Rep. Clarence Cannon, discussing the budget resolution early the next year, said Congress "paid no attention to it." Ibid. (January 13, 1949): 279.

5. Ibid. (May 26, 1949): 6903.

6. Ibid. (August 4, 1950): 11822.

7. Ibid. (May 2, 1950): 6187.

8. For accounts of the development of backdoor spending techniques, see Allen Schick, "The Appropriations Committees Versus Congress," paper delivered to the annual meeting of the American Political Science Association in San Francisco, September 2–5, 1975, pp. 4–5; and Richard F. Fenno, Jr., *The Power of the Purse: Appropriations Politics in Congress* (Boston: Little, Brown and Company, 1966), pp. 98–108.

Schick identified four kinds of backdoor spending in "Backdoor Spending Authority," *Improving Congressional Control over the Budget: A Compendium of Materials,* Senate Government Operations Subcommittee on Budgeting, Management and Expenditures (March 27, 1973): 293–301.

9. 86 Stat 1324, Section 301(b).

10. The vice chairmen from the Senate were Russell B. Long, chairman of the Finance Committee; John L. McClellan, chairman of the Appropriations Committee; and Roman L. Hruska, a Republican member of the Appropriations Committee. Herman T. Schneebeli, the ranking Republican on the Ways and Means Committee, was the vice chairman from the House.

11. HR 7130, S 1541.

12. Transcripts of the meetings of the Senate Government Operations Subcommittee on Budgeting, Management and Expenditures (June 28 and July 18, 1973).

13. *Cong. Rec.* (March 19, 1974): S 3841–3843.

14. Ibid. (December 4, 1973): H 10585. Whitten's bill was HR 10961.

15. Interview, June 7, 1974.

16. 88 Stat 297.

CHAPTER 3

1. Interview, March 3, 1975.
2. Interview, August 28, 1974.
3. Senate Budget Committee meeting, March 5, 1975.
4. *Cong. Rec.* (May 14, 1975): H 4002.
5. Interview, March 4, 1975.
6. House Budget Committee meeting, March 18, 1975.
7. Ibid.
8. Interview, May 15, 1975.
9. Interview, May 18, 1975.
10. Interview, May 9, 1975.
11. Conference committee meeting, May 7, 1975.
12. Interview, May 14, 1975.
13. *Cong. Rec.* (September 22, 1975): H 8935–8941.
14. Ibid. (September 29, 1975): H 9227–9242.
15. House Budget Committee, *Second Concurrent Resolution on the Budget: Fiscal Year 1976* (October 31, 1975), H. Rept. 94–608: 99.

16. *Cong. Rec.* (November 11, 1975): H 10940.
17. Senate Budget Committee meeting, November 5, 1975.
18. Office of Management and Budget, statement, July 2, 1976.
19. Joint press conference, July 1, 1976.

CHAPTER 4

1. Interview, May 6, 1976.
2. Interview, May 4, 1976.
3. Senate Budget Committee meeting, April 1, 1976.
4. Ibid.
5. Section 301(d) (4) of the budget reform act (88 Stat 297) provides that Budget Committee reports accompanying first budget resolutions shall allocate the resolution's revenue total among major revenue sources. The Senate Budget Committee's report for the first resolution for fiscal 1977 (S. Rept. 94–731) includes the revenue breakdown on pp. 6–7.
6. House Ways and Means Committee meeting, March 8, 1976.
7. Senate Finance Committee meeting, February 24, 1976.
8. Senate Finance Committee meeting, February 25, 1976.
9. House Ways and Means Committee meeting, March 8, 1976.
10. House Budget Committee, *Views and Estimates of Standing Committees of the House* (March 22, 1976).
11. House Budget Committee meeting, March 31, 1976.
12. Office of Management and Budget, statement (March 23, 1976).
13. Lynn of OMB responded with a statement dated April 29, 1976, that included this line: "A majority in the House of Representatives proved today that, when push comes to shove, they are much more inclined to break the American taxpayer than they are to give the American taxpayer a break."
14. *Cong. Rec.* (April 9, 1976): S 5318–5321.
15. Letter of June 15, 1976.
16. *Cong. Rec.* (June 16, 1976): S 9574–9575.
17. Ibid. (April 9, 1976): S 5326.
18. Ibid. (June 21, 1976): S 10007–10009.
19. Ibid. (July 20, 1976): S 11987–11989.
20. Ibid. (July 30, 1976): S 12922.
21. Ibid. (August 5, 1976): S 13568–13569.
22. Ibid. (September 16, 1976): S 16019.

23. Ibid. (September 16, 1976): S 16014.

24. This thought was developed by a senior staff member of the Joint Committee on Internal Revenue Taxation in an interview on December 14, 1976.

25. *Cong. Rec.* (September 8, 1976): S 15434–15441.

26. Ibid. (September 22, 1976): H 10802–10814.

27. Ibid. (July 22, 1976): H 7667.

28. Ibid. (June 28, 1976): H 6887–6894.

29. Ibid. (August 3, 1976): H 8205–8217.

30. House Budget Committee, *Second Concurrent Resolution on the Budget: Fiscal Year 1977* (September 1, 1976), H. Rept. 94–1457: 4.

31. Ibid.: 5.

32. House Budget Committee, *Third Concurrent Resolution on the Budget: Fiscal Year 1977* (February 8, 1977), H. Rept. 95-12: 82.

33. *Cong. Rec.* (February 21, 1977): S 2804.

34. House Budget Committee meeting, February 3, 1977.

35. Ibid.

36. Senate Budget Committee meeting, April 26, 1977.

37. Ibid.

38. *Cong. Rec.* (April 26, 1977): H 3554.

CHAPTER 5

1. *Cong. Rec.* (March 22, 1974): S 4284.

2. Interview, May 14, 1975.

3. *Cong. Rec.* (April 26, 1977): H 3557.

4. John W. Ellwood and James A. Thurber, "The New Congressional Budget Process: The Hows and Whys of House–Senate Differences," prepared for the *Praeger Reader on the U.S. House of Representatives* (1976): 33–34.

5. Senate Budget Committee, *First Concurrent Resolution on the Budget: Fiscal Year 1976* (April 15, 1975), S. Rept. 94–77: p. 109, vote 21.

6. Ibid., p. 106, vote 10; p. 107, vote 14; and p. 108, vote 16.

7. *Cong. Rec.* (April 26, 1977): H 3554.

8. Ibid. (April 30, 1975): H 3497.

9. Office of the White House press secretary, statement, May 13, 1976.

10. *Cong. Rec.* (January 28, 1976): S 728.

11. Resolutions as passed by the House and Senate, rather than as reported by the Budget Committees, were analyzed because the

House Budget Committee often made substantial amendments to its budget resolutions on the House floor after reporting them.

12. *Cong. Rec.* (May 5, 1977): H 4067.

13. Interview, May 12, 1977.

14. Interview, May 13, 1977.

15. Interview, March 1, 1977.

16. The bills were S 327 and S 36.

17. *Cong. Rec.* (May 19, 1975): H 4191.

18. Letter to Rep. Melvin Price, chairman of the House Armed Services Committee, August 14, 1975. In Ibid. (September 24, 1975): H 9067.

19. Several Senate Budget Committee members, especially Republicans, complained that current policy built inflation into the budget and left the committee little opportunity to challenge the increasing costs of government services.

20. Interview, September 16, 1976.

21. Letter to Giaimo, reprinted by the House Budget Committee, *Views and Estimates of Standing Committees of the House* (March 15, 1977): 375.

22. *Cong. Rec.* (April 26, 1977): H 3562.

23. Ibid. (April 8, 1976): S 5294.

24. Interview with Ullman, August 28, 1974.

25. Interview, September 10, 1974.

26. Interview, September 11, 1974.

27. House Budget Committee meeting, March 31, 1976.

CHAPTER 6

1. *Cong. Rec.* (March 19, 1974): S 3844.

2. William M. Capron, associate dean of the John F. Kennedy School of Government at Harvard University, examined the CBO for the Commission on the Operation of the Senate, which published his study in *Congressional Support Agencies*, a 1976 committee print. The staff of the House Commission on Information and Facilities reported its findings in *Congressional Budget Office: A Study of its Organizational Effectiveness*, issued on January 4, 1977, as J. Doc. 95–20.

3. Interview, February 21, 1975.

4. C. William Fischer, "The New Congressional Budget Establishment and Federal Spending: Choices for the Future," *National Tax Journal*, vol. 29, no. 1 (March, 1976): p. 12.

5. *Setting National Priorities,* an annual publication of the Brookings Institution, Washington.

6. House Commission on Information and Facilities, *Congressional Budget Office:* pp. 18–19.

7. Senate Budge Committee, *Second Concurrent Resolution on the Budget: Fiscal Year 1976* (November 12, 1975), S. Rept. 94-453: 95.

8. Commission on the Operation of the Senate, *Congressional Support Agencies:* p. 79.

9. Congressional Budget Office, *Inflation and Unemployment: A Report on the Economy* (June 30, 1975).

10. *Washington Star* (June 30, 1975): p. A7.

11. *Cong. Rec.* (October 29, 1975): S 18892.

12. Speech to the National Economists Club, October 21, 1975.

13. Interview, May 7, 1974.

14. Interview, February 21, 1975.

15. House Appropriations Committee, *Supplemental Appropriations for Fiscal Year 1976*: Part I, p. 48.

16. Ibid., p. 60.

17. Ibid., p. 74.

18. Ibid., pp. 82–83.

19. Ibid., pp. 54–55.

20. House Appropriations Subcommittee on the Legislative Branch, *Legislative Branch Appropriations for 1977:* pp. 1080–81.

21. Interview, February 17, 1977.

22. House Commission on Information and Facilities, *Congressional Budget Office:* p. 1.

23. House Budget Committee hearing, June 2, 1977.

24. Interview, January 26, 1977.

25. Commission on the Operation of the Senate, *Congressional Support Agencies:* p. 82.

26. House Appropriations Subcommittee on the Legislative Branch, *Legislative Branch Appropriations for 1978:* p. 399.

27. House Commission on Information and Facilities, *Congressional Budget Office:* p. 20.

28. Commission on the Operation of the Senate, *Congressional Support Agencies:* p. 82.

29. Interview, December 30, 1976.

30. Interview with six CBO budget analysts, January 12, 1977.

31. Interview, January 4, 1977.

32. House Appropriations Subcommittee on the Legislative Branch, *Legislative Branch Appropriations for 1978:* p. 393.

33. Information supplied by the CBO's budget analysis division.

34. Interview with Guy McMichael, general counsel of the Senate Veterans' Affairs Committee, January 12, 1977.

35. Congressional Budget Office, *Five-Year Budget Projections: Fiscal Years 1978–1982*, December 1976.

36. Senate Budget Committee, *Tax Expenditures: Compendium of Background Material of Individual Provisions*, March 17, 1976.

37. HR 10760.

38. S.J.Res. 121.

39. *Cong. Rec.* (February 4, 1976): S 1233.

40. Section 202(f) (2).

41. Commission on the Operation of the Senate, *Congressional Support Agencies:* p. 81.

42. House Commission on Information and Facilities, *Congressional Budget Office:* p. 1.

43. Interview, February 17, 1977.

44. Special Staff Working Group under the Direction of Samuel Cohn, *1976 Budget: Alternatives and Analyses*, April 15, 1975.

45. Congressional Budget Office, *Budget Options for Fiscal Year 1977*, March 15, 1976.

46. Congressional Budget Office, *Budget Options for Fiscal Year 1978*, February 1977.

47. Interview, March 21, 1977.

48. Congressional Budget Office, *The Food Stamp Program: Income or Food Supplementation?*, January 1977.

49. *Cong. Rec.* (December 9, 1975): H 12172.

50. Ibid. (December 9, 1975): S 21475.

51. Ibid. (December 11, 1975): H 12421.

52. Ibid. (December 9, 1975): S 21476.

53. Ibid. (March 19, 1974): S 3833.

CHAPTER 7

1. Office of Management and Budget, *The Budget of the United States Government: Fiscal Year 1978:* 420–421.

2. Office of Management and Budget, *Current Budget Estimates: April, 1977* (April 22, 1977).

3. Barry M. Blechman, Edward M. Gramlich, and Robert W. Hartman, *Setting National Priorities: The 1976 Budget* (Washington: The Brookings Institution, 1975), pp. 197–207.

4. *Cong. Rec.* (April 29, 1976): H 3637.

5. Ibid. (September 17, 1975): S 16128.

6. 88 Stat 297, Section 301(d) (4).

7. Senate Budget Committee, *First Concurrent Resolution on the Budget: Fiscal Year 1977* (April 3, 1976), S. Rept. 94–731: 6–7.

8. 88 Stat 297, Section 301(d) (6).

9. Office of Management and Budget, *Special Analyses: Budget of the United States Government: Fiscal Year 1978,* "Special Analysis F": 128–130.

10. Stanley S. Surrey, *Pathways to Tax Reform* (Cambridge: Harvard University Press, 1973), p. 4.

11. *Cong. Rec.* (May 14, 1975): S 8165.

12. Press conference, July 1, 1976.

13. *Cong. Rec.* (September 15, 1976): S 15870.

14. Senate Budget Committee meeting, April 11, 1975.

15. *Cong. Rec.* (April 29, 1975): S 7101.

16. Ibid. (September 18, 1975): S 16247.

17. Ibid. (September 23, 1975): H 9030.

18. Ibid. (June 14, 1976): H 5773.

19. Ibid. (June 14, 1976): H 5769.

20. Ibid. (June 28, 1976): S 10789.

21. Interview, February 17, 1977.

22. The functions are community and regional development and education, training, employment, and social services.

23. *Cong. Rec.* (September 9, 1975): H 8484.

24. House-Senate conference committee on first budget resolution for fiscal 1978, meeting of May 11, 1977.

25. The bill was HR 5901, passed over the president's veto by votes of 379 to 41 in the House on September 9, 1975, and 88 to 12 in the Senate on September 10.

26. The bill was HR 4222, passed over the president's veto by votes of 79 to 13 in the Senate and 397 to 18 in the House on October 7, 1975.

27. Congress enacted S 3210 over the president's veto by votes of 73 to 24 in the Senate on July 21, 1976, and 310 to 96 in the House on the following day. On February 19, 1976, the Senate voted, 63 to 35, to override a veto of HR 5247—short of the two-thirds necessary to override a veto.

28. Interview, August 30, 1976.

29. *Cong. Rec.* (April 29, 1976): H 3619–3631.

30. Ibid. (April 27, 1977): H 3646–3652.

31. Ibid. (April 27, 1976): H 3455.

32. Interview published in the *Political Observer,* a newsletter published by the Coalition for a Democratic Majority, May, 1976.

33. Interview in October, 1975, with Reuben McCornack, director of the Council on National Priorities and Resources.

34. Senate Budget Committee meeting, October 25, 1977.

35. *Cong. Rec.* (October 25, 1977): S 17681.

36. *Setting National Priorities: The 1976 Budget,* p. 211.

37. For purposes of fixing outlays as a percentage of the national economy, the Brookings authors looked at the gross national product that would result from an economy at full employment—an unemployment rate of 4 percent. In 1976, outlays were 18.7 percent of the full-employment GNP—although they were a higher percentage of actual GNP because the economy was depressed. In 1970, outlays were 20 percent of full-employment GNP.

38. *Setting National Priorities: The 1976 Budget,* pp. 210–20.

39. Ibid., p. 229.

40. Congressional Budget Office, *Budget Options for Fiscal Year 1978,* February 1977.

41. Interview, February 17, 1977.

42. Congressional Budget Office, *Advance Budgeting: A Report to the Congress* (February 24, 1977), pp. 1–2.

43. *Cong. Rec.* (February 18, 1976): H 1125.

44. House Budget Committee, *Congressional Control of Expenditures,* January 1977, p. 126.

CHAPTER 8

1. *Cong. Rec.* (May 1, 1975): H 3557.

2. House Appropriations Committee, *Views and Estimates on the Budget Propsed for Fiscal Year 1977,* report to the House Budget Committee, March 15, 1976.

3. House Budget Committee, *Views and Estimates of Standing Committees of the House* (March 15, 1977): 41.

4. *Cong. Rec.* (March 22, 1974): S 4314.

5. Ibid. (September 17, 1975): S 16128.

6. Ibid. (September 17, 1975): S 16134.

7. Temporary Select Committee to Study the Senate Committee System, *The Senate Committee System—Jurisdictions, Referrals, Numbers*

and Sizes, and Limitations on Membership: First Staff Report (July, 1976):
88.

8. *Cong. Rec.* (September 30, 1975): H 9286.

9. Interviews with a dozen staff members of the House and Senate Appropriations Committees were conducted in the winter of 1976–77. The staff members requested that their identities not be revealed.

10. All figures in this paragraph represent budget authority, which is what appropriations bills provide. Typically the Appropriations Committees make decisions about budget authority, and their staffs then compute the resulting outlays for the current fiscal year.

11. *Cong. Rec.* (March 15, 1977): H 2079.

12. Ibid. (November 14, 1975): H 11206.

13. The Appropriations Committee amended HR 14773, which was passed by the House on September 20, 1976 (Ibid.: H 10498–10502, 10559) and ultimately enacted. See House Appropriations Committee, *Making Improvements in the Survivor-Benefit Program for Retired Military Personnel* (September 17, 1976), H. Rept. 94–1458, Part 2.

The committee opposed HR 4105, which was killed by the House on the same day *(Cong. Rec.:* H 10493–10496, 10557–10558). See House Appropriations Committee, *Recalculation of Retired or Retainer Pay to Reflect Later Active Duty* (September 17, 1976), H. Rept. 94–1435, Part 2.

14. The appropriations bill (HR 14236) included a proviso that its spending levels for ERDA would not take effect until Congress enacted the authorization bill. When Congress failed to enact the authorization bill before the beginning of the new 1977 fiscal year, it had to enact a continuing resolution (HJRes 1105) providing funds to operate ERDA pending enactment of the regular authorization. Ordinarily, continuing resolutions merely provide that the funding level will be that of the previous year or of an appropriations bill that has passed the House but not the Senate. But in this case, the resolution provided that the 1977 funding level was that set by the already-enacted appropriations bill. Thus it effectively removed the proviso that the authorization bill had to come first.

15. House Budget Committee, *Views and Estimates of Standing Committees of the House* (March 15, 1977): 42.

16. Senate Appropriations Committee, *Allocation of Budget Totals*

to Subcommittees for Fiscal Year 1977 (June 8, 1976), S. Rept. 94–933: 1.

17. Interview, September 21, 1976.

18. House Budget Committee meeting, February 28, 1975.

19. Interview with Kenneth A. McLean, staff director of the Senate Banking, Housing and Urban Affairs Committee, October 19, 1976, regarding the report of March 15, 1976.

20. Interview with Donald G. Henderson, deputy chief of the staff of the Senate Foreign Relations Committee, November 10, 1976.

21. Interview with Dale R. Stansbury, an economist with the Senate Agriculture Committee, October 12, 1976.

22. Senate Armed Services Committee, *Authorizing Appropriations for Fiscal Year 1977 for Military Procurement, . . .* (May 14, 1976), S. Rept. 94–878: 7.

23. *Cong. Rec.* (September 29, 1976): H 11620–11621.

24. The original bills were S 2710 and S 3037 (clean water) and S 2150 (solid waste). The clean water bills ultimately were replaced by a substitute, floor amendment No. 2231, on September 1, 1976. The solid waste bill was replaced by a substitute bill, S 3622, which was reported on June 25 and became floor amendment No. 1964 on June 30, 1976.

25. *Cong. Rec.* (March 9, 1977): S 3783. SRes 106 provided the waiver for S 427, which authorized new public works programs.

26. The legislation was HR 10138, and the Interior Committee's request for a waiver was SRes 495. The Budget Committee expressed its opposition in *Disapproving a Waiver of Section 402(a) of the Congressional Budget Act* (August 20, 1976), S. Rept. 94–1159.

27. *Cong. Rec.* (October 9, 1975): H 9977.

28. Ibid. (November 14, 1975): H 11206.

29. See p. 149 of this chapter.

30. *Cong. Rec.* (October 28, 1977): S 18037–18052.

31. The jurisdiction of the House Ways and Means Committee and the Senate Finance Committee extends far beyond taxes. They also are responsible for programs—many of them entitlements—related to health and welfare. As such, they function as authorizing committees as well as tax committees.

32. The legislation was HR 10210.

33. Interview, August 30, 1976.

34. *Cong. Rec.* (July 21, 1976): H 7533–7554.

35. Ibid. (September 8, 1976): S 15436–15438.

36. Interview, September 2, 1976.

CHAPTER 9

1. Louis Fisher, *Presidential Spending Power* (Princeton: Princeton University Press, 1975), p. 150.

2. Louis Fisher, "The Politics of Impounded Funds," *Administrative Science Quarterly,* September 1970, p. 373.

3. 33 Stat 1257 and 34 Stat 48.

4. U.S., Bureau of the Budget, *First Budget Regulations,* Circular No. 4, July 1, 1921.

5. 64 Stat 595.

6. Fisher, "The Politics of Impounded Funds," pp. 364–365.

7. Ibid., p. 366.

8. Ibid., p. 370.

9. Ibid., p. 371.

10. Fisher, *Presidential Spending Power,* pp. 152–153.

11. Allen Schick, *The Impoundment Control Act of 1974: Legislative History and Implementation* (Washington: Congressional Research Service, February 27, 1976), p. 4.

12. Fisher, *Presidential Spending Power,* p. 201.

13. During the period of most intense impounding, the public debt limit was set at $465 billion by the same law (86 Stat 1324), enacted on October 27, 1972, that set up the Joint Study Committee on Budget Control.

14. 64 Stat 765. The Administration interpreted "other developments" to mean almost anything, including a decision by itself that the program was not necessary. The reference to "other developments" was deleted by the budget reform act.

15. Article II, Section 1.

16. A comprehensive account of the court cases can be found in Louis Fisher, *Court Cases on Impoundment of Funds: A Public Policy Analysis* (Washington: Congressional Research Service, March 15, 1974).

17. Georgia v. Nixon, *The U.S. Law Week,* Vol. 42, No. 13, p. 3193.

18. Train v. City of New York, *The U.S. Law Week,* Vol. 43, No. 32, p. 4209.

19. The Senate version of impoundment control legislation was S 373, passed on May 10, 1973. The House passed its version, HR 8480, on June 27, 1973.

20. For a section-by-section analysis of Title X, see Schick, *The Impoundment Control Act of 1974.*

21. Elmer B. Staats, letter to the speaker of the House and the president pro tempore of the Senate, December 4, 1974.

22. Legislation (HR 17505) enacted on December 21, 1974, upheld Ford's rescission proposal No. R75–5, submitted to Congress on October 4, 1974.

23. Deferral No. D75–146 was submitted to Congress on January 30, 1975.

24. This was rescission proposal R75–73, transmitted to Congress on January 30, 1975.

25. SRes 23, passed by the Senate on March 13, 1975, overturned deferral D75–107, which Ford reported to Congress on November 26, 1974.

26. Schick, *The Impoundment Control Act of 1974*, p. 10.

27. *Cong. Rec.* (February 25, 1975): H 1054.

28. The Senate passed SRes 69 on April 24, 1975.

29. 88 Stat 671.

30. The program was authorized by Section 235 of the National Housing Act (12 USC 1715z, et. seq.).

31. Office of Management and Budget, *The Budget of the U.S. Government: Fiscal Year 1974*, p. 119.

32. Deferral D75–48.

33. H. Doc. 93–391.

34. SRes 61.

35. Staats v. Lynn, Civil Action No. 75–0551.

36. 31 USC 665(d) (2).

37. 89 Stat 173.

38. R76–7 and R76–8.

39. R76–50.

40. HJRes 499, which became 89 Stat 225.

41. SRes 205.

42. R75–3 through R75–7.

43. In the 94th Congress, such legislation was introduced by Sen. Walter F. Mondale as S 2392 and by Rep. Robert F. Drinan as HR 2434.

44. Rep. Max Baucus introduced legislation (HR 3827) that would have allowed the House and Senate, acting jointly, to overturn a rescission. GAO, in a letter from Elmer B. Staats to Brock Adams dated November 20, 1975, recommended that a resolution of disapproval be effective if passed by either the House or the Senate, just as deferrals are overturned.

45. Interview, February 17, 1977.

46. R77–4 through R77–12, submitted on January 17, 1977.

47. HR 3839.

48. Actually, Congress could rescind only $453 million of the total. The Navy, without OMB's knowledge, had obligated the other $268 million even before the president proposed the rescission.

CHAPTER 10

1. *Cong. Rec.* (March 19, 1974): S 3832.
2. Ibid. (December 4, 1973): H 10581.
3. Interview, August 5, 1976.
4. Senate Budget Committee hearing, October 21, 1975.
5. Statement, October, 1975.
6. Ford vetoed HR 5559 but signed HR 2166, which became P.L. 94–12.
7. House Budget Committee meeting, August 26, 1976.
8. *Cong. Rec.* (May 1, 1975): S 7258.
9. Senate Budget Committee meeting, April 27, 1977.
10. Interview, August 5, 1976.
11. Interview, July 30, 1976.

CHAPTER 11

1. According to D. B. Hardeman, a long-time aide to the famous speaker, Rayburn never said, "Go along to get along"—at least not in so many words. The quote, Hardeman said, was a fabrication of the *Dallas News,* which frequently tried to malign the speaker. In fact, Hardeman said, Rayburn merely told a breakfast of freshmen representatives that two paths lay before them—one of actively trying to follow their party's leadership and one of consciously seeking reasons to oppose the leadership. Those who followed the former path, Rayburn said, would increase their chances of enjoying the favors that the leadership could dispense.

2. The lone exception was routine. In 1976, the second resolution for fiscal 1977 directed the House Ways and Means and Senate Finance Committees to report a tax cut bill. But the committees already had begun work on such legislation, and the reconciliation section of the budget resolution merely reflected the certainty that Congress would enact a tax cut.

3. Speech to the American Political Science Association convention in Washington on September 1, 1977.

4. Ibid.

BIBLIOGRAPHY

Presidential-Congressional Relations

Binkley, Wilfred E. *President and Congress,* third revised edition. New York: Vintage Books, 1962.

Neustadt, Richard E. *Presidential Power.* New York: John Wiley & Sons, Inc., 1960.

Polsby, Nelson W. *Congress and the Presidency.* Englewood Cliffs, N.J.: Prentice-Hall Inc., 1971.

Schlesinger, Arthur M., Jr. *The Imperial Presidency.* Boston: Houghton Mifflin Company, 1973.

The Federal Budget

Fisher, Louis. *Presidential Spending Power.* Princeton: Princeton University Press, 1975.

Ott, David J., and Attiat F. Ott. *Federal Budget Policy.* Washington: The Brookings Institution, 1977.

Setting National Priorities. Washington: The Brookings Institution, annually from 1970 through 1977.

Surrey, Stanley S. *Pathways to Tax Reform.* Cambridge: Harvard University Press, 1973.

Wildavsky, Aaron. *The Politics of the Budgetary Process.* Boston: Little, Brown and Company, 1964.

Congressional Budgeting

Fenno, Richard F., Jr. *Congressmen in Committees.* Boston: Little, Brown and Company, 1973.

————. *The Power of the Purse: Appropriations Politics in Congress.* Boston: Little, Brown and Company, 1966.

House Budget Committee. *Congressional Control of Expenditures.* Washington: Government Printing Office, January, 1977.

Wilmerding, Lucius. *The Spending Power: A History of the Efforts of Congress to Control Expenditures.* New Haven: Yale University Press, 1943.

Congressional Budget Reform

Ellwood, John W., and James A. Thurber. "The New Congressional Budget Process: Its Causes, Consequences, and Possible Success." In Susan Welch and John Peters, eds. *Legislative Reform and Public Policy.* New York: Praeger Publishers, Inc., forthcoming.

———. "The New Congressional Budget Process: The Hows and Whys of House-Senate Differences." In Larry Dodd and Bruce Oppenheimer, eds. *Congress Reconsidered.* New York: Praeger Publishers, Inc., 1977.

Fisher, Louis. "Congressional Budget Reform: The First Two Years." *Harvard Journal on Legislation,* Vol. 14, No. 3 (April 1977), 413–457.

Schick, Allen. *The Congressional Budget Act of 1974: Legislative History and Analysis.* Washington: Congressional Research Service, Feb. 26, 1976, 75–94 S.

———. *The Congressional Budget and Impoundment Act: A Summary of its Provisions.* Washington: Congressional Research Service, Feb. 5, 1975, revised Sept. 24, 1976, 75–33 S.

———. *The First Years of the Congressional Budget Process.* Washington: Congressional Research Service, June 30, 1976, 76–121 S.

Impoundment

Fisher, Louis. *Court Cases on Impoundment of Funds: A Public Policy Analysis.* Washington: Congressional Research Service, March 15, 1974, 74–61 GGR.

———. "The Politics of Impounded Funds." *Administrative Science Quarterly,* September, 1970, pp. 361–377.

Schick, Allen. *The Impoundment Control Act of 1974: Legislative History and Implementation.* Washington: Congressional Research Service, Feb. 27, 1976, 76–45 S.

Congressional Budget Office

U.S., House, House Commission on Information and Facilities. *Congressional Budget Office: A Study of its Organizational Effectiveness.* Washington: Government Printing Office, Jan. 4, 1977, H. Doc. 95–20.

U.S., Senate, Commission on the Operation of the Senate. *Congressional Support Agencies.* Washington: Government Printing Office, 1976.

INDEX